Praise for *The Unexplainable*

A new call to community, spending fifty days in the Scripture together, opening your own divine invitation to become a part of God's grandest plan in history. Erica Wiggenhorn's delightful passion shines through this study as she brings the early church to life! You're going to love it!

BECKY HARLING
International speaker, coach, and author of *How to Listen So People Will Talk*

Erica Wiggenhorn has done a masterful job of revealing the lessons we can learn from the early church. The format of this study is engaging and the application questions are soul-searching. Invite some friends to go on this journey with you. This study will transform your life.

CAROL KENT
Speaker and author of *When I Lay My Isaac Down*

Erica Wiggenhorn has written a Bible study on the book of Acts that will take you deep into the historical setting while challenging you to live an unexplainable life as a part of the greater Christian church. Take your time and soak in every question and reflect on every commentary she has written—I guarantee you'll be glad you did!

GARY KEITH
Lead Pastor, Life Bible Fellowship Church

The Unexplainable Church takes us back to the beginning and uncovers the power and presence the early disciples experienced as they followed Christ. Each lesson is an invitation to walk in that same power and wonder. Erica does a great job laying a strong biblical foundation while keeping it practical for such a time as this.

DEBBIE ALSDORF
International speaker and author of *Deeper* and *The Faith Dare*
Founder of Design4Living Ministries

Erica Wiggenhorn gives us story, backstory, all the delicious details we love. She helps us dig deep into the mission of the church, its history—even its drama—and brings it to life. You can find your own story there, too.

RHONDA RHEA
TV host and author of twelve books, including the coauthored novel *Turtles in the Road*

As you study your way through Acts 13–28 you will see the power of the gospel, that it can't be stopped, diluted, or quieted by any attack, scheme, or deception of the enemy. The power of the gospel changed the known world through the early church. Erica gracefully yet powerfully reminds us that God is still using His people to take that gospel to our family, friends, and communities.

STEPHEN ENGRAM
Senior Pastor, Desert Springs Community Church
Executive Director Southwest Church Connection, CBA America

This illuminating Bible study connects the past, present, and future for you as you study the ten lessons of *The Unexplainable Church*. You will thrive in your Christian life as you live out the gospel of Christ through the journeys and testimonies of the apostle Paul. A blueprint of life for you to follow is presented in these pages.

JON R. WALLACE
DBA President, Azusa Pacific University

Erica Wiggenhorn has done it again! She guides you on an incredible fifty-day journey that will change your life, refresh your soul, and deepen your understanding of the gospel and God's grace. I have personally fallen in love with the book of Acts as never before.

SUSAN MILLER
Author, international speaker, and founder of Just Moved Ministry

With careful insight and thoughtful questions, Erica challenges the reader to enlist all of the senses in studying the beginnings of the early church and the incredible impact with the message of the cross. The author has skillfully woven solid biblical text, authentic stories, and practical application, which I believe will bring significant transformation to those who engage with this study. It is a brilliant resource to learn more about the early church and how it relates to our role in church history.

CYNTHIA CAVANAUGH
Author of *Live Unveiled* and *Unlocked*
Founder of Women Emerge

the Unexplainable CHURCH

REIGNITING THE MISSION OF THE EARLY BELIEVERS

A 10-WEEK BIBLE STUDY OF ACTS 13–28

ERICA WIGGENHORN

MOODY PUBLISHERS

CHICAGO

Scripture quotations are from the ESV˙ Bible (The Holy Bible, English Standard Version˙), copyright © 2001 by Crossway, a publishing ministry of Good News Publishers. Used by permission. All rights reserved.

Map on pages 254-255 copyright © 2009 The Moody Bible Institute of Chicago.

Edited by Pam Pugh
Cover Design: Dean Renninger and Erik M. Peterson
Interior Design: Erik M. Peterson
Author photo: Suzanne Busta

Library of Congress Cataloging-in-Publication Data

Names: Wiggenhorn, Erica, author.
Title: The unexplainable church : reigniting the mission of the early
  believers : a 10 week Bible study of Acts 13-28 / Erica Wiggenhorn.
Description: Chicago : Moody Publishers, 2017. | Includes bibliographical
  references.
Identifiers: LCCN 2016059262 (print) | LCCN 2017018633 (ebook) | ISBN
  9780802495495 | ISBN 9780802417428
Subjects: LCSH: Bible. Acts, XIII-XXVIII--Textbooks.
Classification: LCC BS2626 (ebook) | LCC BS2626 .W539 2017 (print) | DDC
  226.6/0071--dc23
LC record available at https://lccn.loc.gov/2016059262

ISBN: 978-0-8024-1742-8

We hope you enjoy this book from Moody Publishers. Our goal is to provide high-quality, thought-provoking books and products that connect truth to your real needs and challenges. For more information on other books and products written and produced from a biblical perspective, go to www.moodypublishers.com or write to:

Moody Publishers
820 N. LaSalle Boulevard
Chicago, IL 60610

1 3 5 7 9 10 8 6 4 2

Printed in the United States of America

To Eliana—"My God has answered"—indeed you are an answer to our prayers! May you share the Answer in your generation.

To Jonathan—"Jehovah has given"—indeed you are a gift to us! And may you share the gift of Jesus with your generation.

Your father and I will have no greater joy than to see the Unexplainable Church living on through you.

CONTENTS

A DIVINE INVITATION

"While they were worshiping the Lord and fasting, the Holy Spirit said, 'Set apart for me Barnabas and Saul for the work to which I have called them.'"
—Acts 13:2

This study begins with an invitation. A divine call. A whisper from the Holy Spirit in the depth of our souls that says, "Separate yourself for the special work I have planned for you." There is a flutter in our hearts as He bids us to become one with His purpose. An excitement over what grand adventure may await us. Then questions. Possibly fear. Uncertainty and insecurity creep in, interrupting the sacred stirring within. To which voice will we listen? Which call will we heed?

I'm getting ahead of myself. Acts 13 is not the moment Paul and Barnabas first received their call. Their story began many years and pages back in Scripture. However, the bid to *begin the work* comes now. Long before this moment, Paul and Barnabas made a decision. They chose to surrender to the leading of the Holy Spirit in their lives, no matter where He might send them or what He might ask them to do. This moment of decision occurred first, *an acceptance of the divine invitation*. Once they accepted, the Holy Spirit guided them into relationship with the right members of His church to adequately prepare and equip them. After this time, they were ready to begin the work.

God accomplished their preparation through the study of the Scriptures, development of daily disciplines, the witness of the Spirit's work in and through the lives of other believers, fellowship with Christ Himself, and—this is key—through the other members of the Christian church. For Paul and Barnabas to begin their missionary journey with confidence, they had to resolutely understand they were not being sent out alone. The early church was going before them in prayer, standing alongside them in faith, and following behind them and awaiting their return home in joyful anticipation. The unexplainable church in Antioch and Jerusalem was inextricably tied to the invitation given to Paul and Barnabas.

And the church continues to be inseparably tied to every divine call since. The wonder of the Holy Spirit is that while He calls us individually to live unexplainable lives, He works collectively through the body, bidding the realization of the unexplainable church. The early believers understood their interconnectedness to one another. They found it inconceivable to fulfill the call of Christ apart from each other as members of the Christian church at large.

You, dear one, have this divine invitation as well.

The Holy Spirit has chosen you for a special work. He bids you to become one with Him. But you cannot do it alone. You were not meant to figure it all out by yourself. Hopefully this truth will soothe some of your fears and insecurities. You and I were meant to be threads within the beautiful tapestry called the unexplainable church, the body of Christ Himself. Knitted and knotted together, indivisibly tied to our brothers and sisters around the globe, yet each one individually fulfilling their own special work.

The early believers provide ten lessons to help us understand this fully. These lessons equip and prepare us to *begin the work.* My prayer is that you will accept your own divine invitation. You will discover that you are not alone and will believe in God's faithfulness to provide all you need to be able to fulfill the call He has placed on you—and in that you will rest, listening in your stillness. It seems counterintuitive, I know. But from the beginning of the story we learn God's perfect timing in all things, His clear communication when to act, and His merciful provision once the time for work begins.

As we open the book of Acts beginning in chapter 13, Paul and Barnabas are called to their first missionary journey. Initiated by the Holy Spirit, the church at Antioch comes alongside them, confirming the call. As we step into their sandals and experience the wonder and work of the Holy Spirit on these dramatic pages of Scripture, you and I are invited to take our own journey. As we travel alongside these men, we will be challenged to open our hearts and minds to listen to our own divine invitation, surrender to the Spirit's bidding, and allow the awakening in our hearts to become a flame of obedience to whatever He may call us to do.

"For we are his workmanship, created in Christ Jesus for good works, which God prepared beforehand, that we should walk in them."
—Ephesians 2:10

MAKING THE MOST OF THIS STUDY

"But by the grace of God I am what I am, and his grace toward me was not in vain. On the contrary, I worked harder than any of them, though it was not I, but the grace of God that is with me."
—the apostle Paul, 1 Corinthians 15:10

I have been meditating on this verse while writing this study. How does the grace of God work harder within us? How do we promote its fruit in our lives? Can we accept the grace of God as an intellectual assent and not experience any of its effects? Many Christians rest in the assurance of God's grace to take them to heaven, yet experience little of its ramifications in their daily lives. Or they yearn for more. There is a stirring in their soul, ushering them to experience the fullness of God's grace in their lives. But how?

This fifty-day journey is an invitation to walk alongside a man who never got over the awe and wonder of God's grace. For years he had sought God's favor through a religion of works, spiritual disciplines, knowledge, and service. Then he met Jesus, and after approximately a decade of understanding Jesus as the Messiah, he finally came to the realization of the fullness of His grace. And he was never the same again. Rather than resting on a bed of laurels at the gift of grace he had been given, he strove even harder to ensure that God's grace to him was not in vain. He accepted the divine invitation and most likely met his Savior with a clear conscience and no regrets.

My prayer in studying this portion of Scripture is this: May God reignite the awe and wonder of His grace within each of us. As we pursue Him with everything we have, may His grace abound so lavishly over us that we will never be the same. May we race with anticipation to accept our divine invitation and discover all that God has for us in living out the mission of the unexplainable church. And may *the world* never be the same.

The story of Acts 13–28 holds this truth regarding the unexplainable church: *whatever comes against it, the gospel prevails.* The story of the unexplainable church heralds the atoning power of Christ and the power of His gospel over all sin and death. Let me say that again: all sin. It prevails against injustice, racism, greed, evil, jealousy, economic disparity, corruption, and hate—along with every sin that seeks to destroy it. The one who conquered sin and death through the tremendous tragedy of the cross and the triumph of the resurrection leads the unexplainable church both now and in the ages to come. Our mission as believers in Jesus is to spread the message that God's grace is greater than all. And for others to see its working in our lives.

So if victory is so certain, then where do you and I fit into the church? Why the divine invitation to participate in its preservation and expansion? Because it is God's very design that, through fellowship and service within this unexplainable church, God's grace wields its effects over our lives. Our divine invitation is issued through the church, carried out by the aid and fellowship of the church, and results in the strengthening and spread of the gospel message. Jesus Himself said that the world would know He came from God when His church actively loved one another. The divine invitation is inextricably tied to the unexplainable church.

The early believers held one mission: sharing the grace available through Jesus Christ. This mission united people of different races, religious practices, political affiliations, ethnic traditions, and social classes. This mission spread across the ancient world in a quarter of a century. This mission, the kingdom of Jesus Christ, turned the world upside down. And it is our mission today: to share the powerful, life-altering grace of the Lord Jesus Christ. Will we accept it?

So here is my invitation. Will you join me on this fifty-day journey asking God to awaken within us an awe and wonder of Him, His Word, and His grace? May God reignite within us a fresh vitality as we travel through the expansion of the unexplainable church, witness the power and transformation in the lives of the early believers, and ponder our own divine invitations. May we, like Paul, never be the same. With God's Word, you hold within your hand a divine invitation, etched before time began, and sealed with the shed blood of our King. He bids you to come. May we stand alongside one another in this fifty-day journey, as we encourage one another with trembling hands, maybe out of excitement or possibly fear, to muster the courage to open it.

To maximize the learning time and allow you to listen to God, begin your study time with prayer, inviting the Holy Spirit to speak to you. Also, try to study on a daily basis. This allows ample time to contemplate the content and develop a habit of getting alone with God regularly, strengthening your relationship with Him.

Beginning on Day 2, each day's session starts with a thematic title and Bible passage that will take you about twenty to thirty minutes to complete. Begin your study time by reading the passage in its entirety. Read the daily passage aloud. I've used the English Standard Version as my main text, but you may of course use any version you're comfortable with. If you find yourself confused by a question's wording, referencing the English Standard Version for greater clarity should prove helpful. Reading the daily verses will offer a basic overview of that day's Scripture and story before we break it down in greater depth. The more you familiarize yourself with the verses, the more likely you will remember them and allow their truths to penetrate your heart.

Making your way through each daily assignment, you will encounter several questions in blue. These questions can help you stop, pray, collect your thoughts, and write out answers. Writing responses prompts you to slow down and grapple with the Scriptures, and apply them to your life. On certain days, you will notice blue picture frames. These are your invitation to press pause and dwell in the truths presented that day. Draw, write, doodle, or ponder, allowing the Holy Spirit to speak to you in the quietness of your heart. Bible study is not meant to be a task to complete. Instead, it is an avenue for building a relationship with God. Invest time in your relationship with Him.

Some of the blue questions can also be used in small group discussions. The leader's guide for this study indicates which questions work best for groups. You can access this free resource at www.ericawiggenhorn.com.

A bonus for you, Deeper Discoveries, has some extra material that corresponds with each week's study. This is an optional component in which you can dig more deeply into the Scriptures by making cultural connections with the cities in which the Acts narrative takes place. This is another free resource that is especially helpful for those leading or facilitating a small group through this study. It is also available at www.ericawiggenhorn.com.

I am praying for you as you walk this journey. I pray that God will speak to you, transform you by grace and equip you with the truth of His Word. I would love to hear your discoveries, so please visit me at www.ericawiggenhorn.com and tell me about your progress and insights.

Praying for you,

Erica

unexplainable

BEGINNINGS

THE UNEXPLAINABLE CHURCH
VARIOUS PASSAGES IN ACTS

In case you weren't with us for *An Unexplainable Life: Recovering the Wonder and Devotion of the Early Church*—or maybe you were with us but it's been a while—let's start with a brief history lesson. Acts 13 began after the church had been in existence for a period of at least ten years and possibly closer to twenty. We were first introduced to Barnabas back in Acts 4. Neither an apostle nor a deacon, this humble believer became a key player in the growth and expansion of the early church. During pivotal moments, Barnabas came to the rescue and brought peace into difficult circumstances.

Read Acts 4:32–37 and record every detail you discover about Barnabas:

After Stephen suffered martyrdom under Saul's supervision in Acts 7, the believers fled Jerusalem and scattered throughout the Roman Empire. In an effort to find them, return them to Jerusalem, and have them suffer the same trial and sentencing as Stephen, a man named Saul set out from Jerusalem to Damascus. On this journey, Saul received his divine invitation to follow Jesus Christ and become His witness to the Gentiles.

Read Acts 9:1–19 and consider the following:
What question did Jesus ask Saul?

What command did Jesus give to him?

What additional information about Saul's calling is given to Ananias?

How did Saul, who became known by his Gentile name Paul, later describe this call in Galatians 1:15–16?

Acts 9:26–30 explains how Saul and Barnabas first became acquainted with each other. Describe the circumstances below:

According to Acts 11:19–26, how did Paul and Barnabas later become reunited?

Describe in your own words what you think their relationship may have been like:

The church at Antioch was the first international church. Up to this point, it was Jews who primarily comprised the church, along with some Gentile proselytes. Antioch was the first church to admit Gentile converts—and it was located in the third largest city in the Roman Empire, second only to Alexandria and Rome. The city served as the capital of the province of Syria and was located about a dozen miles inland from the Mediterranean Sea along the Orontes River, making it a large commercial center. Populated by people from varying ethnic and religious backgrounds, the citizens of Antioch acquiesced to the expression of new ideas more readily than other less cosmopolitan cities.

How did the Antiochan believers express their desire for unity with their fellow Palestinian believers in Acts 11:27–30?

After this trip to Jerusalem, Paul and Barnabas returned to Antioch, where our story is ready to begin. Both men who faithfully served the Lord for over a decade will now be set apart for a special work, bringing the gospel into global expansion and turning the world upside down.

WEEK 1 | DAY 2
READY, SET, GO!
ACTS 13:1–3

I so often feel like the timeline of my life could be effectively described by the adage "Hurry up and wait!" Can you relate? I feel rushed day to day, yet I'm also filled with hopes and dreams in the depth of my soul to which God whispers, "Hold on, child. Not just yet." Prayers I long to have answered. Trials I'd like to have over. Chapters I'd like to have closed. Waiting, still waiting. I wonder how Paul felt during this expanse of time since Jesus first appeared to him on the road to Damascus. Prone to emotion and the influence of circumstances, did he ever waver in his belief? As the years passed by, did he begin to doubt God would ever give him the green light to go to the Gentiles?

I find it interesting that we are told virtually nothing as to what Paul did during this time. Other than his trip to Arabia where he received instruction from Christ Himself (see Galatians 1:11–18), we only know that he went home to Tarsus. Then Barnabas showed up and invited him to come to Antioch to help disciple the Gentile believers who needed instruction in how to live. Did Paul feel ready at that point? Was he excited or afraid?

I love the fact that God had Paul minister alongside Barnabas for a solid year before they set out together on their first missionary journey. After being separated for so long, God knit their hearts together through service in a thriving church before sending them into difficult circumstances. God's ways and timing are so unexplainably perfect. During that year, the church at Antioch also received incredible teaching and instruction from these two heroes of the faith. This surely prepared the church at large to pray for Paul and Barnabas as well as continue to thrive in their absence.

What two specific roles of leadership are mentioned?

List the names of the five men in these roles and anything else we are told about their background or ethnicity:

In what two activities were they participating when the Holy Spirit spoke?

What did He say?

Three actions take place in verse 3. Write them out below in their order of occurrence:

The diversity of the church in Antioch is reflected in its leadership. We have already been introduced to Barnabas, a Jew from the tribe of Levi, resident of Cyprus, who therefore presumably spoke Greek along with Hebrew. Paul was a Greek-speaking Jew who grew up in Tarsus and became a Pharisee well versed in the Old Testament writings and fluent in Hebrew. Calling Simeon Niger suggests this man was dark-skinned, an African, or both. Lucius also came from Cyrene.

Manaen, identified as having an intimate relationship with Herod the tetrarch, presumably was well-educated in Hebrew as well as current philosophies and religions common to the first century—possibly due to having been raised in the royal court along with Herod.

Togetherness is implied in their worship and fasting. This emphasizes the unity among this leadership. They were also not too busy carrying out the work of the Lord to gather together and worship the one for whom they so tirelessly labored. What a wonderful lesson for us today in our busy lives! It was this practice of worship, along with fasting, that opened the door for the Holy Spirit to speak.

Do you find it difficult to cease attending to your unending duties in order to gather with other believers solely for the purpose of worship? How so?

On a practical level, what are some things from which we could "fast" in order to allow more time in our lives for worship?

Why do you suppose the Holy Spirit chose to reveal His will in this moment of worship rather than in the midst of their labor?

Notice that it was *after* their worship and the Holy Spirit speaking that they prayed. We are always wise to seek confirmation when we feel we have received a directive from God. After the revelation of the Spirit's will, they quite possibly interceded for Paul and Barnabas, asking for wisdom, guidance, and preparation for this special work.

Why might the Holy Spirit have chosen to communicate His plans to the church collectively rather than directly to Paul and Barnabas individually?

How might you have felt if you were Paul and Barnabas at this moment? Or one of the other three men?

God prepared Paul and Barnabas for this moment. They were ready. Through the unity of the leadership at Antioch, they had the prayer covering, the financial provision, and the blessing for their journey. Now, ten years or so after Saul's conversion as he waited for God to put His call into action, the Spirit said to Paul, "Go!"

BLIND DISBELIEF

ACTS 13:4–12

Up to this point in the book of Acts, authentication of the gospel message was accompanied by miracles. It is no wonder, then, that we see Paul perform a miracle. If either Paul or Barnabas harbored any doubt that God was directing their journey, their supernatural ability over demonic power immediately squelched it. This passage of Scripture records Paul's first miracle.

After traveling the nearly fifteen miles from Antioch to Seleucia, Paul, Barnabas, and John Mark boarded a ship and headed for the island of Cyprus. Their first stop on the island was the city of Salamis.

Where did they preach the gospel within this city?

Where did they go next?

Whom did they encounter there and what was his occupation? Who specifically sought his services?

How is Sergius Paulus described?

From a practical point of view, why would Elymas oppose Paul and Barnabas?

What happened to Elymas as a result of his opposition?

What effect did Paul's miracle have on Sergius Paulus?

Roman citizens were appointed as proconsuls by the Senate. Often they were members of the Roman Senate themselves and well educated. This position is contrasted with procurators who were appointed by the emperor. Why he employed Bar-Jesus, or Elymas, is unknown, but it appears other high-ranking Roman officers employed sorcerers or magicians during this time, presumably to give them advice and to predict the future. In spite of his superstitious nature, Sergius Paulus is still called an "intelligent" man.

Interestingly, it was through the miracle of Elymas's blindness that Sergius Paulus came to see and believe the message of Paul and Barnabas.

While his name, Bar-Jesus, means "son of salvation," Paul called him a "son of the devil." Paul doesn't make this accusation until after he "looked intently at him," thereby implying Paul's discernment into his heart by the power of the Holy Spirit. I think Paul's gift of discernment, along with his ability to perform miracles, is meant to alert us to his new role as an apostle. This special gift of discernment is also attributed to Peter on more than one occasion.

Describe Peter's exercise of this gift in Acts 5:1–11:

Describe it again in Acts 8:14–24:

How does Paul describe his apostleship in 1 Corinthians 15:10?

From this moment forward, we see Paul step into the fullness of his calling as apostle to the Gentiles. Remember, it had been several years since he had been called Christ's "chosen instrument to go to the Gentiles" (Acts 9:15). Paul had learned much, labored intently, and sought to remain faithful to Christ. The moment when he was struck with sudden blindness is brought into crystal-clear clarity. Paul is granted the ability to perform miracles and see into the hearts of men. He has the gifts of an apostle. And Paul's first convert on his inaugural missionary journey? A Gentile.

I find it so beautiful that God allowed Barnabas to witness this monumental fulfillment of Paul's divine call. After all, Barnabas was the first believer to bring Paul into the fold in Jerusalem. In faith he embraced the chief murderer of the early Christian church, believing God was able to change the vilest of hearts. Then again it was Barnabas who set out on the hundred-mile trek from Tarsus to Antioch (Acts 11:25–26) to bring Paul to the first Gentile church. Now, after his faithful encouragement to Paul and belief in his testimony, God allows Barnabas to witness firsthand the fullness of Paul's calling.

Do you have someone in your life for whom you have been waiting a long time to see the work of God fulfilled? Maybe this is occurring in your own life. How does Paul's testimony encourage you?

May we, and those whom we have faithfully served, see, believe, and be astonished at the teaching of the Lord!

Note: It's certainly possible Paul was already ministering to Gentile believers in Tarsus before arriving in Antioch. We cannot definitively know this one way or another; however, this passage in Acts 13 is Scripture's first account of Paul functioning fully as an apostle with the ability to perform miracles and exercise discernment.

For more about Antioch in Syria, see Deeper Discoveries at ericawiggenhorn.com.

WEEK 1 | DAY 4
THERE'S NO PLACE LIKE HOME
ACTS 13:13–43

Traveling to Cyprus meant familiar territory for Barnabas. This island was his home, and he no doubt knew many people there. Paul and Barnabas then sailed to Asia Minor, the region that included Paul's hometown of Tarsus, though that town was not included in their trip. Rather, they traveled a hundred miles north from the coast through mountainous terrain to reach Pisidian Antioch (a different Antioch than Antioch in Syria). John Mark left them and returned to Jerusalem before completing this arduous journey. Upon arrival, Paul and Barnabas once again entered a synagogue to share the good news of Jesus Christ with their Jewish brothers.

What did the synagogue rulers invite Paul and Barnabas to do?

What two groups of people did Paul address? See verses 16 and 26.

What did he admonish them to do?

Carefully read through Acts 13:17–23 and circle every action word (verb). Draw an arrow back to the person doing the action (the subject) in the sentence. What do you notice?

How does Paul describe David in Acts 13:22?

Who is David's promised offspring, according to Acts 13:23?

How does John the Baptist compare himself to Jesus in Acts 13:24–25?

Through this whirlwind history lesson, Paul emphasizes God as the initiator and completer of His will for His people Israel. God carried out and fulfilled His plans despite the unbelief and disobedience of His people (see Numbers 14:20–23; Judges 2:1–4; 1 Samuel 8:4–10). Paul brought to mind God's faithfulness and grace toward His people during pivotal moments in their history. This introduction is paramount—because Paul's next section calls the current generation of Jews in Jerusalem to account for their rejection of God's anointed Messiah.

Read Acts 13:26–39.
Note again the two groups Paul's audience contains:

What does Paul call his message?

Of what are the people of Israel currently guilty?

What action did God take in this passage?

In verse 34, Paul cites Isaiah 55. How does this passage of Scripture allude to the Gentiles being included in the promised salvation of the Jews (see especially vv. 5–11)?

How is David contrasted with Jesus in Acts 13:36–37?

What promise is given in Acts 13:38–39?

The promises given to David were made in 2 Samuel 7:1–17. God proclaimed that the throne of David would last forever. Because Jesus rose from the dead never to die again, He was able to fulfill this promise. He was also able to forgive all sins, our past and present sins, both willful and unintentional.[1]

After delivering his explanation of how Jesus fulfilled the Scriptures, Paul now moved into his final point: "Now that you have heard the good news, you must make a decision."

Read Acts 13:40–43.
What warning did Paul issue to his audience?

How did they respond?

How does the Scripture imply that some of them believed Paul's message (see especially verse 43)?

Yesterday we noticed the parallels between Peter's spiritual giftedness as an apostle and how Paul had been given those same abilities. This sermon by Paul also demonstrated the authenticity of his apostleship. The elements of this first recorded sermon by Paul mirror Peter's initial sermon given on Pentecost.

Read Acts 2:22–36 and fill in the following blanks.

Jesus was crucified according to the _____ of God (v. 23).

Both quote a prophecy of David. Read Psalm 16:8–10 and then write out Acts 2:27.

In Acts 13:33, Paul quotes Psalm 2:7. How does Paul tie in David's prophetic words with who Jesus is?

You, dear one, have mined much information from the Scriptures today. I am proud of your diligence! My prayer, as was Peter's and Paul's in their Spirit-filled sermons, is that you are able to grasp how Jesus is indeed the fulfillment of the Law and the Prophets. As Paul later penned, "For all the promises of God find their Yes in him. That is why it is through him that we utter our Amen to God for his glory" (2 Corinthians 1:20). I also pray you were able to see how Paul preached the same message that Peter preached. This is important because as the Acts narrative unfolds, you will discover that Paul was accused of distorting the elements of the gospel message, creating division among the Jewish and Gentile believers.

You and I hold this beautiful message within our hearts today. If we have accepted Christ as our Savior, we have been given every promise of God.

What are we given as a guarantee that we have received the promises of God, according to Paul in Ephesians 1:13–14?

The powerful Holy Spirit enables us to live unexplainable lives. He unites us together to become the unexplainable church. We are entrusted with the message of salvation in our time and place in history. Paul and Barnabas started their first missionary journey by returning "home." Maybe you and I need to be diligent to first share the message right in our own backyard.

Write down the names of one to five people for whom you will pray "to be a witness" throughout the remainder of this study.

WOMEN OF INFLUENCE

ACTS 13:44–52

Yesterday we read how Paul's sermon left the people wanting more. They begged him to return next Sabbath for further instruction. Some of them even sought out Paul and Barnabas afterward. Their hearts were stirred and minds were piqued with interest to hear more about Jesus. We can assume that news of Paul's sermon spread throughout Antioch in Pisidia by what we discover in today's passage.

Read aloud Acts 13:44–49.
Who gathered on the next Sabbath?

How did the Jewish leaders of the synagogue feel about this? What did they do?

How did Paul and Barnabas respond to them? How did they justify their response?

How did the Gentiles respond to Paul's declaration?

I wish the story ended right here with the semi-happy ending of many Gentiles turning to faith and the rejection of the message by many Jews minimizing the joy. However, this next detail, added on to the end of the story, leaps off the page with conviction and application.

Some synonyms for *incited* include *provoked*, *goaded*, *aroused*, and *inflamed*. Did you notice the women were mentioned in the verse before the men? In a culture where women were second-class citizens, it is uncommon that they would be listed first—unless, of course, their influence exceeded that of the men. Being in women's ministry for over twenty years, I can testify how women hold truly remarkable qualities. Women are tremendous networkers and influencers. If something needs to be accomplished, one woman can round up ten others at a moment's notice to help her complete the task. If you want an event to be organized or an action to be taken, get women involved. They will wholeheartedly jump into a task to meet a need and not look back until it's completed.

But there's a flip side to this. Women's hearts are so big they will quickly and easily offer their help when needed. Sometimes, however, our big hearts become overwhelmed by emotion rather than logic. We jump on board due to our feelings. I don't think the women were listed in this passage first because they were the biggest offenders. I think the women were listed first because the Jews, who harbored jealousy, intentionally sought to incite the women. They knew if they could rouse a small number of prominent women and convince them of the danger Paul and Barnabas posed, they would quickly and effectively network throughout the city to take action. In essence, these Jewish leaders used the giftedness and uniqueness of women against them.

As the Acts narrative unfolds, the role of women in each city Paul visits is highlighted. In every church, women play a vital role in its health or its sickness. Their influence is either directly stated or implied, but they are mentioned in every account. What does this mean for you and me today? A pastor I dearly respect has said, "It's the women who bring the family to church." Mother Teresa said, "If you want to change the world, go home and love your family." My husband frequently jokes, "Happy wife, happy life." Ladies, you and I have tremendous influence in our homes and our churches. We may sometimes feel like second-class citizens, but our influence remains.

Before we close our study this week, let's stop and spend some time with our heavenly Father. Sit at His feet and pour out your heart to Him. Record what He reveals to you below:

How does my attitude influence my family? My church?

How does my speech influence my family? My church?

Do my actions demonstrate the love of Christ to my family? To my church?

The incredible truth is that the church will not become unexplainable without the presence of unexplainable women. Our influence effectively undergirds other believers. As the Christian church navigates through an increasingly turbulent culture, we can either shore up the body of believers or shipwreck it. When others emotionally incite us to respond or take action, may we first run to the arms of our Father for guidance.

unexplainably
UNSTOPPABLE

WEEK 2 | DAY 1
THE CERTAINTY OF OPPOSITION
ACTS 14:1–7

One thing anybody who knows me will tell you is this: I despise confrontation. I will avoid it at all costs, even if the price tag is higher than the confrontation itself. It has taken me years to get beyond this fear and realize that it's something I'll never avoid; therefore, I must learn how to handle it with grace and healthy boundaries. My instinct is to run for cover behind my husband. He's a pro at handling confrontation. Paul didn't seem to mind confrontation, either. He never seemed frazzled in the midst of it, and later in Acts we'll see him shrewdly capitalize on it. I don't know if I will ever get to that point in my life, but if you and I are going to live out our divine call, we're going to face opposition.

Read Acts 14:1–7.

Where did Paul and Barnabas go in Iconium and what happened?

What opposition arose while they were there?

What did Paul and Barnabas do as a result?

How did God graciously authenticate their message?

How did the opposition intensify?

How did Paul and Barnabas respond?

While they were forced to move out of the city, they still did not cease to share the gospel message. Instead, they moved to new places to preach some more. When it comes to serving the Lord, opposition is guaranteed. When the Lord begins to do the unexplainable in and through us, the intensity of the opposition will increase. When it really heats up, we may want to quit. We may doubt God is with us. We may focus on the results in the valley rather than remember the command God issued on the mountaintop. We may retreat into a cave all alone instead of continuing the trek.

How do you and I make sure that doesn't happen? What do Paul and Barnabas teach us? Expect opposition. It's not an indictment that you misunderstood the mission. Opposition is greater proof you're engaging the enemy.

Don't let opposition distract you. You'd think that Paul and Barnabas left after the unbelieving Jews incited the crowds. Instead, they spent considerable time there—as a result of the confusion the opponents instilled in the Gentiles' minds.

Trust God to honor the call He placed on you. In the midst of the opposition,

God proved the claims of Paul and Barnabas by allowing them to perform miracles. I'm not suggesting we should necessarily expect God to do this exact thing in our lives today, but if our hearts are pure and our motives are set to exalt Christ, God will guard our testimony and the truth of our message.

For you and me to accept our divine call and live unexplainable lives forming the unexplainable church, we've got to be ready for battle. It's not going to be a walk in the park. It's going to be war, as we read about in Ephesians 6:10–17. We will see Paul face opposition on every side. But we'll also see God carry him through, granting him victory after victory until at last Paul won his greatest victory of all—deliverance unto Jesus and eternal life.

How do you deal with opposition? Use the space below to write out your own prayer to God. Express your fears and concerns and ask for grace to follow Him into any battle He may allow in your life.

THE SATISFIER OF OUR HEARTS
ACTS 14:8–18

After traveling to their hometown regions, somehow Paul and Barnabas ended up in the small, outlying village of Lystra. Though not a prominent city and technically not even part of the Roman Empire, most of its residents spoke the native language of Lycaonia rather than Greek. It's quite unclear why Paul and Barnabas came here since it was not situated along a common trade route or communication line. Perhaps they needed a "backwater village" in which to rest after all the upheaval in Iconium. It also appears that there isn't a synagogue in Lystra because Luke makes no mention of one. Without a common language or religious background, the Holy Spirit empowered Paul to gain the attention of the people through a miracle.

Read Acts 14:8–10.
Describe the condition of the man:

What did Paul do to assess this man's faith?

What did Paul say to the man and what happened?

Look back at Acts 3:1–8. What similarities do you see between this miracle and Peter's?

This first missionary journey of Paul and Barnabas is believed to have lasted anywhere from a year to eighteen months. Yet we are told of only three main events during this entire time—the conversion of Sergius Paulus on Cyprus, Paul's sermon in Pisidian Antioch, and this miracle in Lystra. Surely there were many more stories to tell. So why were these particular stories chosen above the others? These stories of Paul were designed to authenticate his apostleship. His sermon and miraculous abilities and actions mirror those of Peter. While Peter was chosen as the head of the Jewish church, Paul was called to be the chief apostle to the Gentiles (see Acts 9:10–16).

I also think we are being presented with numerous ways that Paul was tested. In Cyprus, Paul and Barnabas faced spiritual opposition through Elymas. In Iconium, they faced emotional opposition through slander and false accusations. Now in Lystra, they are tested in the opposite manner. What will they do when they are flooded with praise?

What temptation did Jesus face in Luke 4:5–8?

Let's take a look at the humility of Paul and Barnabas and their desire for God alone to be exalted.

Read Acts 14:11–18.
How did the crowds respond to the lame man's miraculous healing?

Who did the Lycaonian villagers believe Paul and Barnabas to be?

How did Paul and Barnabas respond to this belief?

How did Paul describe Zeus and Hermes versus the God of Israel?

What evidence did Paul say God provided regarding His existence and His goodness?

Did Paul's explanation convince them to stop trying to worship him and Barnabas?

There was an old legend in Lystra that Hermes had once come down to this village in disguise. When the villagers were inhospitable, he cursed their land. Not wanting to make the same mistake twice, the people jumped into action and were ready to go over the top in honoring Paul and Barnabas. Since Paul likely needed an interpreter to speak to them, he kept his sermon short. He began with what they could see and understand: nature. However, they could not be persuaded.

How does Paul explain nature as evidence of God in Romans 1:19–25?

In what ways do you see people today worshiping "created things" rather than the Creator?

In what way could our efforts to seek man's praise also be considered "worshiping created things"?

Only God truly satisfies our hearts. He alone gives gladness. Every other thing we worship may provide a fleeting moment of happiness, but they are "vain things." In the end, they do not satisfy. God continually draws the hearts of His creation to Himself. In Lystra, it was through a miracle. He is drawing your heart today, friend. He wants you to turn from useless things to understanding Him as the living God who satisfies your heart. Spend some time today sharing the empty, hurting places in your heart with your Father. Ask Him to show you what it might look like to worship Him—even in those broken areas. Record what He impresses upon your heart below:

HE STRENGTHENS OUR SOULS

ACTS 14:19–23

Have you ever been in a situation where you assessed the circumstances and thought, "Well, I've got nowhere else to go but up. Surely it can't get any worse than this"? That may have been how Paul and Barnabas felt in Lystra. However, the events at Lystra that we reviewed yesterday turned from bad to worse. While Paul and Barnabas were trying to convince the crowds that there was only one living God (and they are not it), the Jews from Antioch and Iconium show up. This can only mean more trouble.

What happened in Acts 14:19?

Were they correct in their assessment of Paul's condition according to Acts 14:20?

Some scholars attribute Paul's ability to get up and walk as nothing short of miraculous. The mob left him as good as dead, yet he recovered consciousness, stood up, and walked back into the city. Paul had passed yet another test: physical persecution. He didn't flee in fear. He walked right back into the city where his persecutors most likely were residing for the evening before returning to Antioch and Iconium. So much for fleeing to Lystra for respite!

Look back at Acts 14:20 once more and note where Paul and Barnabas went next:

Read Acts 14:21–23.

Describe what happened there:

Where did they go next?

Why?

How did Paul and Barnabas say we enter the kingdom of God?

What did Paul and Barnabas make sure they did in each city before they left?

Why do you think this is important?

What did Paul and Barnabas do as part of the appointing process?

Why do you suppose they did that rather than just say, "Here are your leaders"?

Considering all the opposition Paul and Barnabas faced in these cities, these infant believers could count on some hard times ahead. No doubt they would face tribulation on account of their faith. In order for their faith to survive, they were going to need some strengthening and leadership. I imagine it was hard for Paul and Barnabas to leave them. No doubt Barnabas, called the Son of Encouragement, felt as though he couldn't encourage them enough before having to depart. Paul likely could've spent years going through the Scriptures with them, strengthening their souls. For them to leave with peace of mind despite their heaviness of heart, they had to feel certain the right men were being left in charge.

Who or what has God used in your life to "strengthen your soul"?

Who or what has God used in your life to encourage you?

In what ways might the establishment of spiritual authority over us as a church collectively guard us from falling away?

Have you ever had to let go and "commit someone to the Lord," relinquishing your influence over them? Describe the circumstance and how it made you feel at the time:

How could prayer and fasting be beneficial to you personally if you had to commit someone to the Lord?

I find it interesting that God did not afford Paul and Barnabas a great spiritual harvest on their journey until *after* they had undergone several tests. I also consider their call to let go, move on, and say good-bye to these believers as yet a fifth test. It would have been natural for them to assume the growth and establishment of these early believers as their sole responsibility. I love how we are reminded that they gave them to the Lord. Into whose hands could a soul be better entrusted?

Maybe there is someone in your life you have been trying to strengthen and encourage for a long time. Maybe you feel that to back away will mean their sudden falling away from the truth. So you have held on tightly, trying to secure the outcome your heart desires. Maybe you've also done everything possible to spare them from tribulation, or stayed involved in their lives when it was time for you to move on. Perhaps you have an unwillingness to allow someone else to exercise spiritual authority over their life.

It's time to commit them to the Lord. It's time to entrust them to the one in whom they have believed and to allow His will to be done in their lives—even if it means some hardship.

Pause today and write down the names of a few of the people you love most in this world. Ask God to search your heart while asking Him the following questions: What do I do to encourage them?

How do I strengthen their souls?

Have I entrusted them to You?

Pray and ask God to show you what it looks like to "commit them" to Him. He is trustworthy to strengthen their souls.

WEEK 2 | DAY 4
A TIME OF JOY AND REST
ACTS 14:24–28

After leaving Iconium, Lystra, and Derbe, Paul and Barnabas made a second pass through the region of Pisidia and Pamphylia. Unlike during their initial route, this time they stopped in Perga and preached there. I love the fact that they shared the gospel and then came back around again to follow up with these new believers. They understood the importance of discipling these young churches. Most of these churches were established in towns where strong opposition to the gospel was manifested the moment Paul began to preach. It was easy to understand how many would initially receive the gospel with joy, but then quickly fall away unless Paul and Barnabas took proper measures to equip them to continue to grow. Think of it: these early believers had no Bible, no pastors per se, and no one to learn from other than the devout Jewish believers who could explain the Old Testament to them. How different it is for us today with countless resources at our disposal to understand the Scriptures.

Now Paul and Barnabas return to their home church in Syrian Antioch. They have quite the arsenal of stories to unload upon their arrival.

Read aloud Acts 14:24–28. Mark on the map where Paul and Barnabas stopped before returning to Antioch.

To whom did Paul and Barnabas tell their missionary stories?

How did they describe God's work with the Gentiles?

Why do you think Luke says a door of "faith" rather than a door of salvation? How would you explain the difference?

Why do you think Paul and Barnabas remained in Syrian Antioch for "no little time" rather than continuing on another missionary journey right away?

I'm sure a spectacular celebration ensued when Paul and Barnabas returned! Who knows if the Antioch church had received any communication from the pair during their journey. Can you imagine the awe of the Gentile believers in Antioch hearing how Paul healed the lame man and struck Elymas with blindness? Or how Paul was stoned and left for dead only to get back up and walk away? This is some missions report! The most astonishing part of their stories is how many turned to the Lord and received the gospel message, both Jews and Gentiles. It affirmed that indeed God set Paul and Barnabas apart for this missional work. The Lord moved mightily among them!

After all the exploits were recounted, the trauma of the persecution retold, and the rejoicing complete, it was time to rest—and these men needed a long time to rest. They had been on the move for over a year, possibly closer to two years, facing constant opposition in every town. Within their church family, these men received both spiritual and emotional refreshment as they shared the joys and sorrows of their journey.

This, I believe, is what makes the church unexplainable. It is within our family of faith that we are able to celebrate and rest. We can share both our ups and downs as fellow sojourners following our Lord.

In what way is your local church a place of rest and refreshment for you?

Describe when you shared a time of joy or sorrow with a fellow believer:

How does knowing that other Christians face opposition like you knit your heart to theirs?

What are some practical ways you could make your home a place of rest or refreshment for other believers in your faith family?

How do you intentionally carve out time for rest in your own life?

Paul and Barnabas had been so busy traveling, preaching, and dodging stones they didn't really have much time to process all that had happened to them and through them. They lived in the moment, full of the Holy Spirit, and moved on from place to place in awe of God's ways. Personally, once I return home to a familiar and safe place after an intense time of ministry, I hit a brick wall emotionally and physically. However, for Paul and Barnabas, another form of opposition is on the horizon.

> To learn more about the region of Galatia, go to Deeper Discoveries at ericawiggenhorn.com.

WEEK 2 | DAY 5
THE LETTER OF GRACE
ACTS 15:1–21

In the midst of the celebrating, some visitors arrive—and they are going to rain on Paul's parade. These men were from Judea, the region where Jerusalem was located.

Read Acts 15:1–5.

According to these men, what must Gentiles do to be saved?

How did Paul and Barnabas react to this?

What course of action did they deem to be wise in order to seek resolution?

On their way to Jerusalem, what did Paul, Barnabas, and the others do?

How did these Samaritan and Syrophoenician brothers respond?

Once they arrived in Jerusalem, which group opposed them?

This is a serious question that needed to be settled immediately. If Gentile believers could not receive Christ without being circumcised first, that could become quite a hindrance to their accepting the message. Maybe to us this question seems silly, but to the Jewish people, circumcision was serious business.

Read Genesis 17:1–14.
What was the promise God made with Abraham in this covenant?

What was to be the sign of the covenant?

How long was the covenant to last?

According to this covenant, who else must be circumcised besides the Jewish people?

How did God feel about anyone who was not circumcised?

Because the covenant was to be an eternal covenant for all generations, God chose the sign of the covenant to occur on Jewish males at precisely the place where future generations were conceived. Anyone who did not follow God in circumcision was not under the covenant promise. No wonder it was inconceivable for Gentiles to be welcomed into Messiah's arms without being circumcised.

Read Acts 15:6–11.

Who participated in this debate?

Who took the lead in the debate?

What evidence did Peter cite as proof that the Gentiles were welcomed into God's covenant promises?

Finish these statements made by Peter in the ESV in this passage:
". . . having cleansed their hearts by _____. . . .
But we believe that we will saved through _____
_____ just as they will."

Now read Acts 15:12–21.

How did the apostles and elders respond to Peter's speech?

Who spoke next and what did they say?

Who spoke last and what did he suggest they do?

There is a lot going on in this debate among the apostles and elders, so let's see if we can shed some light on their thought processes. I believe one of the most beautiful aspects of this passage is Peter's explanation of how a person gains salvation: by faith in God's grace demonstrated in the death and resurrection of Jesus Christ. I also love how he reminds all the assembly that God "knows the heart." While we, in our humanness, often form opinions of others based on their outward appearance and actions, it is God who sees our true selves—even the pieces of our heart we can't see or are too afraid to behold. Chris Tomlin put it this way in his song "Indescribable" —"You see the depths of my heart and You love me the same." Who is like our God who loves us in spite of ourselves? No wonder they all fell silent.

What James says is equally compelling. By quoting Amos 9:11–12, his point emphasizes that inclusion of the Gentiles in no way contradicts Scripture. In Jewish thought, no matter how miraculous an experience seemed, if it did not align with the Scriptures, it lost credibility. Adherence with the Word of God was the litmus test of accuracy. Alignment with Old Testament prophecy put the ultimate stamp of approval on any decision made.

What I find equally beautiful is that in all three points made in this case, every man cited the work of God. Peter asserts that *God poured out* His Holy Spirit on the Gentiles in Cornelius's home (see Acts 10). Paul and Barnabas reported the signs and wonders *God did* through them. Then James detailed what *God spoke* through His prophets. None of the members in this debate seem to have recalled anything Jesus said concerning Gentiles or their mission to take the gospel to the ends of the earth. The conclusion is clear: salvation is a work of God through grace and not the result of the performance of man.

What did Paul write later to the believers in Ephesus regarding their salvation in Ephesians 2:4–10?

Now read Acts 15:19–21.

If Gentile salvation is a work of God, then why do you suppose James includes these commands that appear to be "works"?

I think we need to look carefully at the order. James isn't saying, "Stop doing these three things and then you can be saved." Rather he is asserting, "If you have become a follower of Jesus, it is best if you cease participating in these behaviors." He is talking to Gentiles who are *already* saved. These are not requirements to achieve salvation; these are directives you willingly submit to in light of your salvation. Scholars vary on their reasoning as to why James included these particular directives, but the consensus is that these activities were often included in pagan temple worship. In other words, once you accept Christ, you should not continue to worship other gods as well. This seems obvious to us in our monotheistic Christian background, but we need to remember that most of these Gentiles probably worshiped multiple gods simultaneously. To worship God by adding Him to their already existing pantheon of personal worship would not have been strange to them.

In what ways do you see people today worshiping God plus someone or something else?

Spend some time allowing the Holy Spirit to speak to your heart today. Do you have someone or something in your personal pantheon that needs to be dethroned? Write out a prayer of commitment below:

unexplainable

GRACE

WEEK 3 | DAY 1
SEEMINGLY GOOD
ACTS 15:22–28

Have you ever had someone rain on your parade? I don't know why it is so, but it seems that in the wake of great celebratory moments of life there is always a trial or tragedy riding in on the tail of it. Maybe it's spiritual warfare, maybe it's just life, or maybe it's a combination of the two, but it seems to be the norm in my experience. It was also the norm for Paul, who, after stepping fully into his calling as apostle to the Gentiles, is about to face a massive schism within the early church.

The Jerusalem council, presided over by James, Jesus' half brother, faced the most essential question of the Christian faith: how are people saved? A sect of Pharisees, whom Paul called the Judaizers, insisted that all people, Jews and Gentiles, must observe Jewish laws and customs, including circumcision, in order to receive salvation. The Jerusalem council, however, decided that salvation was issued by grace alone and works were not a factor. This represented a radical shift in thought for the Jewish people who had for centuries achieved atonement and favor from God through observance of the Law and the sacrifices. Not needing to "do" anything to achieve God's favor would be extremely hard for them to embrace.

Read Acts 15:22–28 aloud from the ESV and circle the phrase that is repeated three times.

This verb phrase in the Greek is *doxeō* with the noun form being *doxa*.[2] The primary definition of *doxa* is honor, renown, and glory, especially divine. The definition further denotes the idea of what one thinks about a person or thing, to recognize a person or thing for who or what it is, or their reputation, honor, or renown.[3]

Now read aloud Acts 15:22–28 (ESV) and substitute the phrase "seemed good" with "showed what God is like." In other words, insisting that salvation is achieved solely by grace gives a clearer picture of who God is and what He is like.

It also shows that by choosing trustworthy men to deliver His Word through Judas and Silas, God is a shepherd of His people; that He is a God of unity by bringing all His servants to one accord; and that the Holy Spirit reveals and echoes the character and work of God.

Why do you suppose it would have been important for men from the Jerusalem church to accompany Paul and Barnabas back up to Antioch with the letter from the Jerusalem council?

Describe the level of unity evident in Acts 15:22:

What do you suppose is the meaning of "leading men among the brothers"?

What are some characteristics you esteem in church leadership and why?

By what name do the members of the Jerusalem church address the Antiochan church members and why would this be important?

One evening my husband and I were out running an errand and we received a text message. My husband handed me his phone with furrowed brows. "What's wrong?" I asked, worried that something had happened at home. "Read this," he said, thrusting the phone in front of me. "I don't like the tone of this message." "Tone?" I replied. "You can't tell what the tone of a text message is. Stop reading into it."

No matter how carefully the Jerusalem council worded their letter, it still could be misinterpreted or misconstrued. Sending messengers to deliver the contents face-to-face and answer any questions was the most effective means of dispelling any further miscommunication. I also think it served a greater purpose as well. The trek from Jerusalem to Antioch in Syria was about three hundred miles. For members of the Jerusalem church to make such an arduous journey, they demonstrated their desire and commitment to solidarity with the Antiochan church.

Let's face it, unless you have been to a place, interacted with the people who live there, heard their stories and shared their daily life experience, it is difficult to truly love them with the same depth. Not because we don't want to, but because we are sensory and relational creatures, and once we have engaged on that level, the experience becomes indelibly printed upon our hearts and minds. These Judaizers had damaged the hearts and minds of these young Antiochan believers by their disturbing presence. In their wisdom, the church leaders knew they now needed a healing presence to restore unity.

Who do you know who offers a healing presence to those around them? What are some ways they do so?

To whom could you offer a healing presence?

I believe one of the greatest ways we show others who God is and what He is like is through a ministry of presence. Pausing our frenetic schedules or casting aside our electronic devices long enough to sit across a table from someone and share an encouraging word brings honor to God in ways that are truly underestimated. When you and I, namely the church, take the time to engage with people in their daily lives, we become unexplainable in a busy, selfish and distracted world.

WEEK 3 | DAY 2
THE BIG DEAL ABOUT DOCTRINE
ACTS 15:28–31

I suppose none of us should be surprised by how frequently the church gets caught up in issues of doctrine and practice. We can see from this passage of Scripture that the dispute started early within the history of the church. Up until this point, nearly all members of the Christian church were Jews or Jewish proselytes. So naturally they embraced Jewish doctrine and practice wholeheartedly. Even the Samaritans shared Jewish roots, although their ethnicity varied. Paul is bringing in a new group of Jesus followers now and they know nothing of Judaism.

While the issue had been settled that salvation through Jesus was received by grace and grace alone, how these two very different groups of people were going to become unified remained a challenge. They spoke different languages, had different religious backgrounds and experiences, practiced different social norms, and held very different levels of knowledge and understanding of the Old Testament Scriptures. Culturally each group looked down on the other. Integrating them into one unified church was going to be difficult. Unexplainable, maybe?

No wonder the members of the Jerusalem council recommended some ground rules to help facilitate their unification. Let's look carefully at what those ground rules were and discover how we might be able to apply these admonitions to our own lives.

Read Acts 15:28–31.
List the four things from which they were asked to abstain:

1.

2.

3.

4.

How did the believers in Antioch respond to these recommendations?

Now I've read about fifteen different opinions in regard to these four items. Various commentators hold a different slant as to why the council chose these four items in particular. Rather than examine each of these individual practices in and of themselves, I think we would do well to try to understand the purpose behind them. I would imagine the last one is a no-brainer, but the first three, which have to do with eating, sound pretty strange to us.

Read Acts 2:42 and 46.
Describe a major part of church life with these early believers:

If Jews and Gentiles were going to come together to celebrate communion and share meals, they were going to have to be able to eat from the same table. The council offered suggestions in order for fellowship between the two groups to not be hindered. It wasn't sinful to eat any particular kind of food, but if it caused division or the people of God to separate from each other, then it should be avoided.

How does Paul further expound on this idea in 1 Corinthians 10:23–33?

Essentially Paul is admonishing all Christians to be willing to make concessions for one another in order to facilitate unity. This is completely countercultural to the American way of thinking. In our history we separated from the British crown rather than concede to demands our founders found unacceptable. Today we still consider that giving up our rights is practically un-American. In the early church, however, they realized that waiving their rights for the sake of Christian fellowship was a noble endeavor. More noble than asserting independence.

We have to remember: doctrine has already been established. The teachings of the church were no longer open to debate. That was no longer an issue. What was at stake was the unity of the church. Would these new believers demonstrate a willingness to make a concession out of care and concern for their Jewish brethren? For these Jewish Christians to eat non-kosher foods seared their conscience. They needed time to process all that freedom in Christ Jesus meant. The council is asking these Gentile Christians to offer grace and understanding as their Jewish brothers and sisters wrestled with all that it means to no longer live under the law. They are asking them to give up the preferential and convenient for the sake of unity.

If we're honest, church division occurs more often over squabbles regarding practice than it does over essential doctrine. The music is too loud. There aren't enough hymns. Nobody claps, the worship time is dull. The pastor is too long-winded. The pastor doesn't go deep enough in his sermons. He's too cerebral and not practical. They don't have enough parking spaces. The service time is too early. There aren't enough seats and I don't like sitting next to strangers. The list could go on and on. And if we suggest that rather than point out these problems we just concede to things we object to, suddenly we're accused of heresy. What was a matter of opinion or preference before suddenly elevates to doctrinal divergence.

Could it be that the concessions we make in our churches actually are the very things God uses to make us more like Christ? Could it be that when the music displeases my flesh, but I choose to worship in spite of it, part of my flesh becomes crucified and my spirit strengthened? Shall I choose to notice those around me tearfully responding to the old hymn or hanging on every word spoken by the pastor rather than begrudgingly sitting through a passage of Scripture I already know by heart? Would it not be unexplainable if we wholeheartedly worshiped in spite of the absence of our personal preferences? This is the level of maturity James is calling the churches to live up to. Frankly, I could use a lot of work in this area of my life. How about you?

Here's a challenge. Write down ten things you are grateful for in your church. It could be ten people or ten programs, or even the paint color on the wall. Just find ten things. Then for the next three days bring them daily before the Lord in thanksgiving, asking Him to teach us to dethrone our preferences and exalt Him. A willingness to seek the good of our brother and sister in the church over our personal tastes and desires would be pretty unexplainable, wouldn't it?

THE PLUS SIDE OF PERSONALITY CONFLICTS

ACTS 15:32–41

One of the most amazing things about our God is how He repeatedly brings something good or beneficial out of difficulty. I have seen it over and over so many times, when something goes wrong I begin to look around to see if I can find the blessing that is currently disguised. Now please don't attribute this to my reaction toward deep tragedy. While I still believe God is able to bring something good or beneficial out of it, I don't face horrible events with whimsical spiritual platitudes. I'm talking about misunderstandings, flat tires, and broken cellphones. Regular stuff of life. Not earth-shattering disappointments. Do I believe God is able to redeem even the darkest of tragedies? Yes! But it's not my initial reaction when hearing about them.

Today, we're going to see God bring about good through two issues. In all honesty, they both appeared pretty major at the time as far as disagreements go. But God used them to bring about good in His mysterious, marvelous, unexplainable way! The first disagreement we've already covered: law versus grace. The second we're going to read about. But let's start with the good news first.

Write out Acts 15:32 below:

Judas and Silas had come to the church at Antioch due to a disagreement in the church. Chances are, if the disagreement had never occurred, a Jerusalem council never would have convened, and these two exemplary leaders in the Jerusalem church never would have come.

We know their purpose in coming was to deliver the council's decision that salvation was by grace and not works of the law, but it was also to ensure consistent and correct communication among the fellowship. Furthermore, it was a clear display of Jerusalem's desire for solidarity among all churches, whether they were primarily composed of Jews or Gentiles. We know all these purposes were accomplished, because we're told in Acts 15:33 that this envoy from Jerusalem left in peace.

Another positive result was the further strengthening of the church at Antioch, because Paul and Barnabas saw the need to remain there for a time, offering further teaching in the Scriptures (Acts 15:35). As we will see in the rest of today's passage, Paul's heart was to return to the churches he and Barnabas had established on their first missionary journey. This disagreement, however, caused him to remain in Antioch for a time in order to equip the church through which his future missionary journeys would be funded and supported. Paul understood the importance of discipleship among these Gentile believers who had little to no background in the Old Testament Scriptures.

Read aloud Acts 15:36–41 and record the following:
What did Paul want to do?

What was Barnabas's desire?

What happened as a result of the problem between them?

We spent quite a bit of time on Paul and John Mark's relationship in *An Unexplainable Life*, so I'm not going to retell the whole story. However, it is important to recognize that Paul and Barnabas did not immediately reconcile over this issue. It's hard for me to wrap my mind around the fact that these two spiritual giants couldn't come to an agreement. Honestly, when I see people in church leadership who refuse to come together in reconciliation, I become judgmental. I feel like they're setting a poor example. So let's wrestle this through a bit.

First of all, I'm not sure they went their separate ways in a huff. The Scripture tells us that they were "commended." I think Paul and Barnabas agreed to disagree. So they parted ways. They were both committed to missions and preaching the Word of the Lord; they just felt it was time to do so separately. I'm not suggesting that either was completely without fault, but for Paul to take John Mark along, he would have done so begrudgingly and in a critical spirit, serving as a distraction from the message of grace he was called to deliver. For Barnabas to choose Paul's way over his heart for his cousin quite possibly would have produced deep guilt within Barnabas, distracting him from the message of freedom in Christ he was called to share. So rather than concede one to another, they chose to separate.

The positive result? The missionary movement multiplied. With this new foursome, not only were all the established churches visited and strengthened, but Paul, with the aid of Silas, was able to cover new territory on this second missionary journey, which I can hardly wait to show you. But for now, let's allow the Holy Spirit to do a little soul searching within us.

When disagreements and disappointments come your way, how do you generally react? Why?

When or how have you seen God bring something good or beneficial out of one of these times?

When you see people in church leadership unable to fully reconcile, how does it make you feel?

After reading today's passage, can you see how God may be able to use their differences of opinion to further the kingdom?

Is there someone in your own life with whom you have had a disagreement? Is there something you feel you need to do in light of today's reading?

I find it so interesting that this story about Paul and Barnabas occurs immediately after James's call for concession and unity within the church, don't you? It awakens me to the fact that our enemy will pull out all the stops to create division among us as believers. It also makes me aware that even in disagreements and division, God has a plan to bring something good from it. If you've been nursing a wound or holding a grudge, it's time to let go. A willingness to trust that God has a plan to redeem it is pretty unexplainable.

LOIS'S LEGACY

ACTS 16:1–5

My sister-in-law Amy worked as a waitress while she was in college. One evening my husband's former high school English teacher sat down at her table. She recognized "Wiggenhorn" on Amy's name tag and asked her if she knew a Jonathan Wiggenhorn. "Sure do," she replied. "He's my oldest brother."

"Hmm," muttered Mrs. English Teacher. "How is he these days?"

"Oh, he's great!" Amy responded. "He's been married almost ten years now and he's a doctor."

"A doctor!" the teacher blurted out incredulously. "Jonathan, Jonathan Wiggenhorn, a doctor? Joey's brother?"

"Yep," my sister-in-law assured her with a chuckle. (My husband was not a stellar scholar in high school, though later he excelled in college.)

Regaining her composure, the teacher shook her head and smiled. "Well, that's just great! I never would have guessed that in a million years. Please tell him I said 'hello' and that I'm extremely proud of him!"

There's something indescribably wonderful in the life of a teacher when you reconnect with one of your students after several years and hear how their life has beautifully unfolded . . . especially when you had braced yourself for disappointment. I can't express the joy that wells within me when I connect with former students on Facebook and hear about their lives. I imagine Paul could hardly wait to return to the churches he had established with Barnabas a couple of years prior. And what a treat God had in store for him!

Read aloud Acts 16:1–5 and consider the following:

Why had Paul and Barnabas gone to Lystra and Derbe in the first place (see Acts 14:5–7)?

What had happened in Lystra (see Acts 14:19)?

What had Paul and Barnabas done before leaving these cities (see Acts 14:23)?

Based on what you read in Acts 16:1–5, how effective had these elders been in overseeing the church?

Why do you suppose Paul wanted to take Timothy with them?

What further information do we gain about Timothy in 1 Timothy 1:18 and 4:14?

How about 2 Timothy 1:5–7?

There are some important takeaways here that we don't want to miss. Paul informs us that it was Timothy's grandmother, Lois, who was the first to come to faith in Christ. Lois then passed her faith down to her daughter, Eunice, who then passed it on to Timothy. Notice Timothy's father is not mentioned at all. We are only told that he was a Greek. For all you grandmothers out there, your legacy matters. For all you single moms out there, or married ones with unbelieving husbands, your legacy matters. Paul called Timothy his "true son in the faith." Timothy's legacy started with two devout women, and he grew to become the man to whom Paul wentrusted every church he had founded. Your legacy matters. And so does mine.

We can become distracted by feeling sorry for ourselves if we shoulder the weight of being the spiritual rudder in our home, or we can remember Timothy. You and I have no idea what God has in store for the young men and women in the generation behind us. Will we use the years we have with them wisely? Lois and Eunice remind us that our children's ability to make a tremendous impact on the kingdom of God isn't dependent on our husband's faithfulness or lack thereof. Sure, it plays a part. But it's not an indictment or a guarantee. We have a role to fulfill as well. And we'd be wise to take it seriously.

If you are a grandmother, mother, aunt, or an older sister, in what ways do you pass on your faith to the generation behind you?

Describe in a sentence or two what kind of women you believe Lois and Eunice were:

If there was one thing you were to do differently TODAY in building a legacy of faith within your family, what would it be?

Think of a woman you know who you feel prioritizes this concept of legacy within her family. Pray about approaching her to mentor you.

The truth is that the first church we have been called to strengthen and build is the one that gathers around our own kitchen table. Or maybe, like Mrs. English Teacher's, it's around your desk or blackboard. Even Paul took extra care to disciple "his true son" over and above the thousands of believers he had been called to shepherd. If we are distracted by "other works" than discipling our own children, we need a mentor to steer us back to shore. Your legacy starts with you.

Conclude today by writing a short letter to a young man or woman in your life. Include two to three truths you hope to impress on them through your influence. Sign and date the letter, tucking it away for an appropriate time.

MYSTERIOUS MACEDONIA

ACTS 16:1–10

Yesterday we saw Paul's small missionary entourage begin to grow with the addition of Timothy. I love how God is so faithful to send us exactly whom we need to fulfill the work He has for us. The young and able Timothy not only provided physical aid, but I'm sure his youthful energy also provided a daily reminder to Paul that he would not be young forever and eventually these churches would fall under new leadership. Paul may have wondered for how long he would be able to endure such intense travels. Timothy's presence brought perspective about the future.

I find it interesting that Paul had Timothy circumcised, especially in light of the sharp disagreement he held with the Judaizers back in Acts 14–15. Again, I think we see Paul's heart for his people and his willingness to make concessions for his Jewish brethren in order to facilitate unity. And if Timothy's dedication was ever in question, I'd say this act of obedience put it to rest.

How are Paul's actions in having Timothy circumcised better understood by reading 1 Corinthians 9:19–23?

While some may argue that Paul is contradicting himself here by circumcising Timothy, I disagree. Rather, I think he is precisely demonstrating the attitude that the Jerusalem council asked the Gentile believers to exhibit in light of their Jewish brethren. If Timothy's lack of circumcision would create an obstacle in their ability to preach the gospel to the Jewish people, then Paul logically concluded that the obstacle should be removed. He wasn't forsaking his convictions that Timothy was saved by grace alone, he was making a concession in order to facilitate unity and open the door of communication. Often a tiny line exists between conviction and concession, yet there's a world of difference in its effects.

What are some areas where you see people unwilling to make concessions because they have created convictions in their mind and upheld them as the only biblical stance?

How do some of these convictions create division in the church?

How can we hold on to our convictions, yet still create concessions within the church body as a whole, facilitating unity and opening the door for the further-ance of the gospel?

While this mention of Timothy's circumcision almost appears as an aside in Luke's overall narrative, I think it is of fundamental importance in this part of our story. From here forward, we are going to see Paul begin to take his group of missionar-ies and head into new and unknown territory. The diversity of people who would comprise the Christian church was going to grow—not only in numbers but also in differences. If a willingness to offer concessions out of a desire for unity was not clearly established, it would only mean division, chaos, and factions. A willingness to become all things to all men is pretty unexplainable, isn't it? Maybe it's time that you and I stop wishing everybody were just like us and ask ourselves whose shoes we need to step into to better understand them.

Read aloud Acts 16:5–10 and complete the following chart:

WHERE THEY WENT	WHERE THEY WERE FORBIDDEN TO GO
_____	_____
_____	_____
_____	_____
_____	_____
_____	_____

Circle all the places they went on the map in the back of your study book. Underline the places where they were forbidden to go.

They went east and the door closed. They went north and it closed again. Heading south, God called them west to Macedonia. Interestingly, God would eventually send Paul to both of the areas He had currently forbidden him, but for now he was to go to Macedonia. How exactly the Holy Spirit and Jesus stopped them we are not told. Maybe those directions were also given by a vision as the call to go to Macedonia had been. We cannot be sure. What we can know, however, is that God has a time and purpose for everything and closed doors are not always a work of opposition against us. Sometimes they are the divine guidance of our loving Father.

I also find it interesting that we are given no indication that Paul was frustrated by these events. Paul pressed on in his missionary travels and when God redirected him, he simply turned and took another route, trusting God to lead him where He willed. Ministry still happened along the way. Paul's travels were not a waste of time. He was just stopped in his tracks once he began to cross into territory the Lord did not intend for him to travel at the current time.

Often when I encounter obstacles, my first response is that I have stepped out of God's will. Every step I took to that point is negated in my mind as disobedience or all for naught. I beat myself up wondering how many steps backward I will have to travel before I discover exactly where I got off course. This passage lends itself to a much broader truth, however. Paul and his companions were preaching the Word exactly where God intended, and as soon as they began to venture into an unintended area, God put up a roadblock and intervened. Paul had no idea exactly what his ending destination was to be at this point; he just kept moving forward, waiting for God to tell him where to go next. And that also included where not to go.

> See Deeper Discoveries at ericawiggenhorn.com for more information about Macedonia.

Another area where I fall short is my failure to take any steps until I know exactly where God intends my final destination to be. If I don't fully understand the entire purpose and end result, I'm not ready and willing to begin the journey. This passage reminds us that God can be trusted to continue to lead us on every leg of the journey. And He expects us to venture out in faith even before we have all the answers.

When have you faced an obstacle and wondered if it was God redirecting, or spiritual opposition coming against you?

How do you generally respond when you run into a closed door?

What is an obstacle you are currently facing? How does today's story broaden your perspective?

Is there an area of your life that holds a lot of unknowns, yet you sense God calling you to step out in faith? Talk to Him about your concerns below:

the *unexplainable* WAYS OF GOD

ONE WOMAN WELCOMES THE WORD

ACTS 16:11–15

After several reroutes and closed doors, Paul and his team concluded that God intended for them to go to Macedonia. I shared with you last week my gut-level response when I face closed doors. Today God is going to shed some light on what can happen when we walk through open ones. Just as in the former case, our initial assumptions as to what He is doing may not always be correct.

Read Acts 16:11–15 aloud and consider the following:

Where in Macedonia did Paul first preach?

About how long were they there before Paul first preached (see vv. 12–13)?

To whom did he preach specifically?

How does the Scripture describe the process by which Lydia came to believe?

Based upon Lydia's conversation with Paul in verse 15, how would you describe Lydia's personality?

There are so many little details packed within this short story that we cannot miss. Although their travel to the city occurred quickly and without event, once they arrived, it was several days before Paul first preached to anyone. Paul saw a man in his vision, yet his first convert was a woman—a woman from Asia where he had been forbidden to go by the Holy Spirit. Hmm . . . What is the point of all of this?

Interestingly, there does not appear to be a synagogue anywhere in Philippi, because there is no mention of one. According to Jewish law, if there were ten Jewish men, a synagogue must be formed. If there were not ten Jewish men, then the few there would gather together on the Sabbath at a designated site, which they would call the "place of prayer." Because ceremonial washing was a regular part of Sabbath worship, this would often occur near a natural water source in order for the men to complete these ceremonial rites. This explains why Paul and his companions looked for Jewish men down by the river on the Sabbath.

However, in the gathering he encounters, no men were present, only women. The specific woman who is mentioned is not even Jewish, she is from Thyatira and a worshiper of God. She is presumably quite wealthy as she sold clothing made with purple dye, which was very expensive and worn by the upper class and royalty. Also, we know her home must have been quite large in order to house Paul and his companions after her conversion.

I also think she was a strong leader. Why do I think this is so? Because after her conversion, her entire household was also baptized. This probably included the men who worked under her.[4] She understood Paul's explanation of the Scriptures and was able to communicate it effectively to those with whom she lived and worked. In a culture in which women were regarded only slightly above slaves, for the men to listen to her explanations and believe her was really quite something. Also, the language used in the story suggests that Lydia *insisted* they stay with her. And look at how she posed the question to Paul: If he said, "No," it would mean he didn't really believe her to be a true convert. Surely Paul wasn't going to insinuate that. So she orchestrated the situation in such a way that she couldn't take no for an answer. This is one strong woman to speak to men in such tones in her day and age.

I have to wonder what Paul thought of all this. He had seen a vision of a man, yet his first convert was a Gentile woman. Now we have the beauty of hindsight in that we know the two-thousand-year history that will follow and how the continent of Europe would become the launching pad from which the gospel would spread worldwide, including to our own American soil. Of course Paul knew none of this, only that the Lord had called him to Macedonia to help a man he had seen in his vision. And as our story unfolds, we'll see that Paul's second presumable convert was a slave.

THE WAY TO BE SAVED
ACTS 16:16–24

So far Paul's experience in Macedonia is not at all what he probably imagined based on the vision God had given him. Nevertheless, he saw the Holy Spirit opening hearts and drawing people to Christ Jesus. In this he no doubt rejoiced. However, in the midst of all of this, his heart became grieved because of an encounter.

After finding the place of prayer where worshipers of God would gather for the Sabbath, Paul and his companions went there daily. Each day a poor slave girl would follow them all the way outside of the city chanting the same thing over and over. Eventually it got to the point that Paul couldn't take it anymore. I think Paul's frustration went beyond the simple annoyance of hearing her say the same thing over and over again. The word used for "annoyed" or "irritated" can better be understood as "grieved."[5]

The word used in this text for divination is the Greek word *python*, meaning "a spirit of python," referring to a mythical serpent that guarded the Delphic oracle. According to Greek legend, the python was a symbol of the god Apollo. The people believed it was his spirit dwelling within the slave girl that enabled her to predict the future.[6] So her divination skills in being able to know and understand Paul's message, without actually hearing it for herself first, demonstrated that Apollo was on equal ground as the god whom Paul preached. The "Most High God" we understand to be Yahweh, but in Greek thought it could also mean Zeus. Paul did not have any desire to allow her to equate her god's abilities with his own. In a polytheistic culture, Paul had to be certain that his hearers did not perceive him to be proclaiming another god—he was proclaiming the one and only God.

Second, this poor girl obviously was completely under the control of a demonic spirit, not even realizing what she was saying or doing, robotically following Paul around babbling the same sentences over and over again. Surely this broke Paul's heart to watch and to hear, knowing she was created by the God He served and loved by Him as well. To her masters, she was nothing more than a piece of property to be exploited.

Read aloud Acts 16:16–24.
Whom specifically did Paul address?

What did he say and what happened?

How did her owners respond?

What accusation did they bring against Paul and Silas?

Well that's interesting! I would have expected them to say, "These men drove the spirit of Apollo out of my slave girl!" but none of that is mentioned at all. Instead, they pulled out the race card. "These men are Jews." Anti-Semitism ran high throughout Rome at this time. The Roman Emperor Claudius had expelled Jews from the city of Rome. Part of the Roman imperial cult was to worship Caesar. Since Jews worshiped no one but God, they were targeted by the Roman government. As history tells us, so were Christians for the very same reason. These slave owners knew exactly how to rile the crowd up and they capitalized on it.

It was also against Roman law to worship any god either publicly or privately that had not been accepted and authorized by the Roman government.[7] So not only are they bringing up the anti-Semitism, they are accusing Paul and Silas of introducing a new god to worship. This was only a half truth, as Yahweh was not exactly a "new god." The crowd, in their fury, stripped Paul and Silas of their clothing and began to beat them, then threw them in jail for the night.

Now I have to admit, if I were Paul, I would really be second-guessing myself right now. They have yet to meet this mysterious Macedonian man in their vision. In fact, as far as we can tell, other than Lydia's employees, they have yet to witness to any men at all. Now, after expelling a demon from a slave girl, they are nearly beaten to death and locked away in prison. I would start asking God if I had understood Him correctly. It didn't seem as though anyone in Macedonia was particularly interested in their message and the people's hatred of Jews had been painfully apparent. Why had God sent them here?

How would you have felt if you were Paul at this moment?

Have you ever had a situation in which you felt like you were following God's directions but it ended in disaster or disappointment? What did you learn at that time?

As we will see tomorrow when the rest of this story unfolds, the Holy Spirit was just beginning to stir in the winds of Macedonia. He was going to burst upon the scene in a miraculous way! Maybe you're in your own place of disaster or disappointment right now. Life feels dark and dank, like you're stuck in a dungeon. When you put down your study book today, friend, remember, this story isn't over. The good part is coming. And your story isn't over yet either—so hold on, the Holy Spirit is just beginning to stir.

Find out more about Philippi and Thessalonica at Deeper Discoveries at ericawiggenhorn.com.

A JAILER SET FREE

ACTS 16:25–40

We left off yesterday in the lowest part of our story. Paul and Silas have been beaten and thrown into prison. Today is when the tide begins to turn. I believe the very first verse we encounter is the key to this shift in circumstances.

Read aloud Acts 16:25–31.

Write out Acts 16:25 here:

What suddenly happened?

When the jailer rushed into the prison, to whom did he immediately go?

What question did he ask? Write verse 30 here.

Write out Paul's answer here (v. 31):

When I picture this scene in my mind's eye, all I can do is shake my head in disbelief. Here were these two men, backs ripped open, shoved against a jagged, rocky wall with their hands fastened above them and their ankles below, singing out their hearts to God. No doubt they were unable to sleep due to the pain, yet they chose to praise God—unexplainable! In fact, it is so unexplainable that no one in that prison was asleep. They were all listening to Paul and Silas in utter disbelief. Who in their right mind would be singing in circumstances like this? Who would be praising a God who had allowed such horror into their lives? Of course they were listening—they must have been completely astonished by these two men.

And what does the Holy Spirit do in the wake of their prayers and hymns? He rushes in with a great earthquake, freeing Paul and Silas from their chains. And not theirs only, but every prisoner within the facility. Now while the prisoners were witnessing all this, the jailer remained fast asleep. Until the earthquake. Then suddenly he realized all the prisoners were essentially able to escape, meaning his certain death. In utter horror as to what his future held, he drew a sword to kill himself.

Somehow by revelation of the Holy Spirit, Paul realized what he was about to do and cried out for him to stop. I believe God revealed the jailer's intentions to Paul supernaturally because we are told that he and Silas were in the "inner prison" and after Paul yelling for him, the jailer then rushes in to the section of the prison where Paul and Silas had been chained.

I find his question so interesting. *What must I do to be saved?* How did he know that Paul and Silas had been preaching a means to salvation before being dragged into the prison? Had he heard the slave girl talking about the way of salvation? Had he heard their prayers and songs before he had fallen asleep? How did he know about Paul's message and what he had been preaching? I think this story offers us a couple of great reminders.

First of all, when we choose to praise in the midst of difficulty, God moves. The Scriptures tell us that our God dwells in and is enthroned on the praises of His people (see Psalm 22:3). Could it be that if we spent more time praising God in our daily lives, or even in the difficulty, rather than comparing and complaining, we'd see God moving a lot more often on our behalf? Do we really believe the Scriptures that when we are praising God with our whole heart in spite of our circumstances, He simply cannot stay away?

Second, when we choose to praise in the midst of our pain, people take notice. Our lives become unexplainable and those around us can't help but watch and listen in amazement. Our salvation becomes so visibly obvious and powerful that others start wondering, "How do I become saved beyond circumstances?" and a door opens to share the truth and transforming power of Christ. Why in the world wouldn't we readily and intentionally verbally remind ourselves of the goodness and greatness of our God and His miraculous saving power in the midst of pain and difficulty? What better time is there?

Now read aloud Acts 16:32–40.
What did the jailer do for Paul and Silas after they shared the gospel with him?

Who else was impacted?

What message did Paul receive from the jailer the following day?

How did he respond?

What did Paul do before he left Philippi?

We have to remember how the slave girl's owners had capitalized on the obvious anti-Semitism within the town.

So here Paul departs from his interesting group of believers at the church at Philippi: a wealthy Gentile immigrant woman, a slave girl, and a Roman jailer. Could you get a more disparate group of people? Let's put this in modern terms. Picture a row of chairs or the pew at your church. In file a famous Italian clothing designer, a young girl recently rescued from the sex-trafficking industry, and a middle aged male correctional officer. Sitting side-by-side worshiping together. Pretty unexplainable, isn't it? Have you ever been to a church like that?

The message of the church at Philippi is this: all the labels, misconceptions, hatred, and bigotry that our enemy may use to divide us is no match against the power of Christ to unite us. For years of his life Paul had been a staunch Pharisee and abided by all the restrictions that would entail. Now as Paul hugged his band of converts good-bye in Lydia's living room, he may have prayed something like, "Oh God, how I praise you for this woman, this Gentile jailer, and this beautifully restored slave, all members of Your kingdom." That my friends, is the unifying power we hold within us. And the story of this little church in Philippi is the truest picture of the church I have ever seen.

WEEK 4 | DAY 4
TURNING THE WORLD UPSIDE DOWN
ACTS 17:1–9

As Paul and his entourage trekked the hundred miles from Philippi to Thessalonica, the wonder of grace must have replayed through his mind countless times. How upside down were the ways of God—everything he had once understood about God's favor had been shattered by grace. Understanding the composition of believers in Philippi sheds a whole new light on Paul's letter to them, doesn't it?

> "I thank my God in all my remembrance of you, always in every prayer of mine for you all making my prayer with joy, because of your partnership in the gospel from the first day until now." (Philippians 1:3–5)

Never in a million years as a Pharisee would Paul have ever believed he would join in a partnership with a woman, a Gentile, and a slave girl. Never would he have thanked God for such people. Never would he have experienced joy from knowing such a trio as these. No wonder Paul wrote so much about God's grace—he had been completely undone by it. Who was this God of grace who took the law and turned it upside down like this?

No wonder Paul was so zealous to share with his Jewish brethren. He had been in the dark for so long, believing God's favor had been brought by works and identity as a Jewish man. What freedom Paul had found—what depths of love! No one was incapable of receiving the grace and favor of God.

Read aloud Acts 17:1–5.

Where in Thessalonica did Paul go to preach the gospel?

What specifically did Paul try and explain to his Jewish brethren?

What three groups of people believed Paul's message?

The Jewish prophecies regarding the Messiah spoke of the restoration of the land and David's kingdom, meaning Israel would govern herself again under Messiah's rule. Because they were still subjugated to Rome, it was difficult for the Jewish people to believe that Messiah had come. As Christians we understand that Jesus came the first time to save, by dying on the cross. When He returns again, He will rule and reign. The Jewish people had a hard time splitting these two events.

Pastor Chuck Smith tells the story of the time he was able to meet then–prime minister of Israel, Menachem Begin and their discussion regarding the Messiah:

> I had the opportunity on a couple of occasions to sit and talk with [the prime minister]. I found him a very charming person, and very committed to the Bible. I once told him, "You know, there really isn't much difference in our beliefs. For you believe in the God of Abraham and Isaac and Jacob, and that's the very God I believe in, the One who created the heavens and the earth and everything in it. You believe that the Messiah is coming soon. And I believe that the Messiah is coming too. So the basic difference is that when the Messiah comes, you will say, "That's the Messiah," and I will say, "That's the Messiah." But I will add, "This is the second time He's been here."[8]

When I was in Israel this year, I had a similar conversation with our Jewish tour guide. Over and over I was fascinated by how highly he spoke of Jesus, quoting from the Gospels verbatim. Finally, I flat out asked him, "What is it specifically that makes you doubt that Jesus is the Messiah?"

"How do you say I don't believe that Jesus is the Messiah?" His answer floored me.

"Well, because then you would consider yourself a Christian, would you not?"

His second statement left me scratching my head even harder than his first one. "When Jesus came, he came as your Messiah. But when He returns to rule and reign, He will come as Israel's Messiah." I honestly wanted to stop the whole tour and pull him aside and have about a four-day discussion with him as to what he meant by that, but of course, there were forty other people in our tour group who had their own set of questions to ask. The point is this: Paul had his work cut out for him in trying to reason with his brethren that a Messiah who suffered but did not restore Israel politically could still be the Messiah whom they were expecting.

Read aloud Acts 17:5–9.
What specific emotion did Paul incite in the Jewish religious leaders?

Of what did the Jews accuse Paul specifically?

When they couldn't find Paul and Silas, who did they use as a scapegoat and why?

How many times has vibrant ministry been thwarted due to jealousy? Why is it we cannot celebrate the work of God despite whom He chooses to accomplish it? I find it so interesting that this is the motive they are assigned. It would make so much more sense for it to read, "Then some Jews who were zealous for the law formed a mob" or "Then some Jews who opposed Paul's message formed a mob," but it doesn't say that. It simply says they were jealous. Paul was turning the world upside down and they didn't like it. Interestingly, wasn't that the very thing they expected Messiah to do—turn the world upside down? Or maybe in their mind, right-side up! Yet they denied Paul's Messiah.

These guys were slick. They got some rabble rousers to do their dirty work, disassociating themselves from the uproar. This way "the Jews" couldn't be blamed for rioting. Then they basically took Jason—a leader in the synagogue and Paul's host—hostage and made him pay security money. So, if Paul left town, Jason was in the clear. If he didn't, then Jason would be imprisoned for housing Paul and his companions. They put Paul between a rock and a hard place. While he no doubt wanted to stay in Thessalonica and further teach these new believers, these jealous men forced him to leave.

This whole affair sheds light on Paul's letter to them when he writes: "we wanted to come to you—I, Paul, again and again—but Satan hindered us" (1 Thessalonians 2:18). The "money as security" was likely to ensure the city authorities that Paul would not return. Were Paul to do so, it would mean the authorities could go arrest Jason again. Yet despite Paul's sudden necessary departure, this band of believers had continued to grow. We know for a time Paul sent Timothy to them (1 Thessalonians 3:2), no doubt to encourage and comfort them.

And so here we have it again, a church crossing gender, ethnic, and racial lines banding together under the banner of Christ Jesus. Not only that, but suffering persecution together and standing strong—pretty unexplainable! In our own world with its schisms over gender, race, politics, and religion, we can learn much from these early believers. The grace of the Lord Jesus be with us all!

THE WONDER OF THE WORD

ACTS 17:10–15

I have noticed something in all these cities so far. It seems as though Paul and Silas are the ones entering the synagogues and engaging in debates. Timothy is hidden somewhere in the background. We know he is there, because he is mentioned on occasion, and in Paul's later letters he is included in the greeting. But in the heat of the battle he never seems to be around. I wonder why this is so? If he came as their "helper" then maybe he is in the marketplace gathering supplies, or working for someone to earn money for them. Maybe due to his youth, Paul sought to protect him and keep him out of trouble. Maybe Paul disassociated with him purposefully when they entered towns so when he and Silas were thrown out, Timothy remained undercover enough that he could return to the town to check on the fledgling churches. Or, maybe it was a little bit of all three.

What we do know is that after Paul and Silas were thrown out of cities, Timothy was often left behind to help encourage and pastor these young churches. It's almost like he misses out on all the exciting stuff, though. Where is he when people are being baptized? When important citizens are falling at Paul's feet in repentance because they have been so undone by grace? What a bummer to be in the background in such events. Of course, he's also missing the riots and floggings too.

The point is this: when we feel left in the background, we still matter. Just because our service isn't dramatic doesn't mean it doesn't make a difference. If there were no Timothys hanging behind to do the daily work of teaching others what it means to follow Jesus in their city, with their problems, and community issues, how many churches would survive? If all we had to grow was the occasional evangelist passing through town or the big name speaker, how many of us would truly stay committed? Timothys matter. Behind-the-scenes folks matter. Mentors matter. Sunday school teachers and small group leaders matter. Pastors matter. We need their encouragement, input, and teaching regularly to continue to grow.

Why do you think we tend to measure success in ministry based on the size of it?

After the drama of Philippi and Thessalonica, the faithful trio departed for Berea, which was about sixty miles away. Again, quite a journey on foot.

Read aloud Acts 17:10–15 and answer the following:
Where did Paul go to preach first?

How are the Bereans described?

What action did the Bereans take in response to Paul's message?

What three groups of people responded to Paul's message?

Who or what disrupts Paul's work?

Who leaves Berea and who stays behind?

One thing that strikes me as so beautiful in all these accounts is the openness of the Jewish synagogues. Somebody shows up and they are brought into the fold and given an opportunity to share their story and expound on the Word. How different our Western churches are today. We wouldn't dream of allowing someone to speak in our churches without vetting them to ensure they're doctrinally sound or at least recommended by someone we trust (which is a sound practice). The Jews of the first century, however, loved to debate. They felt the process helped them clarify their thinking and wrestle through the Scriptures in a way that led to greater learning and understanding. And—this is vital—they also knew their Scripture soundly enough to pick up on teaching that might be false or dangerous.

There is an old story of a rabbi who walked into a synagogue and began to expound on the Torah. All those in attendance sat raptly listening and nodding in assent. The rabbi complained, "Won't anyone disagree with me so we can engage in debate?" Today, we don't like debate. We don't want to leave anything open-ended. And honestly, we are sadly aware that too many church attenders don't know the Scriptures well enough to actually listen with discernment and engage in debate or discussion.

How different it would be if we had to be on our guard with everything taught to us. What if we went to church with the expectation that we were to go home and search through our Bibles to determine the accuracy of what had just been shared? How would that change our engagement with the Scriptures and the way we paid attention on a Sunday morning? Unfortunately, we don't live in a culture that is committed to poring over the Word of God and examining it. We expect instead to walk into church and be fed by our favorite pastors with a glittering silver spoon.

No wonder Paul warned again and again to be on guard against false teachers. No wonder he exhorted Timothy over and over again to preach the Word, teach the Word, hold fast to the Word, and so on. These early Jewish believers had to understand the Scriptures or they could easily have been led astray. Becoming a follower of Jesus meant becoming an active learner. Paul had no patience for ignorance or spiritual laziness.

In what ways do you see spiritual laziness in our culture?

How do you personally guard yourself against false teaching?

When was the last time you truly examined the Scriptures to see if what your pastor or Bible teacher said was true? Describe the circumstances:

I love the story of the Bereans. I love how we are told they examined the Scriptures daily to see if what Paul said was true. If we're going to live unexplainable lives, we've got to know this life-transforming Word. If we're going to stay strong in spite of persecution and opposition, we have got to have its promises hidden in our heart. Spend some time today talking to the Lord about your commitment to study His Word. Record what He reveals to you below:

an
unexplainable
LEGACY

WEEK 5 | DAY 1
TO MARKET HE GOES
ACTS 17:16–21

The jealous Jews from Thessalonica continued to follow Paul and his entourage to Berea. Paul's inability to remain in the province of Macedonia quickly became evident. He needed to travel some distance to allow the dust to settle. So they sent him off to Athens. Greek through and through, this city encompassed every cosmopolitan sway and whim a single city could hold. Noted for its erudite philosophers and endless opportunities for sensual experience, Athens embodied a culture entirely antithetical to Hebrew thought. When Paul entered the city, his heart was grieved.

Because I grew up in Los Angeles, I can somewhat relate to Paul's feelings. So many sights to take in, people everywhere, immense wealth and evidence of human accomplishment, yet a prevailing lack of purpose amid all the hustle and bustle. Many editorialize, bemoaning current events, yet offer no real solutions. Hollywood moguls flaunt their wealth and beauty, yet often give the impression of being more about these fleeting things than about making the world a better place. People everywhere are chasing money, fame, materialism, and a big break so they feel like they have "made it." Or they aimlessly seek a moment of pleasure to forget the dreariness of their lives. It reminds me of when Paul says, "But we always carry around this treasure in jars of clay." In the midst of all of these *important* people, suddenly Paul may have felt small, like an average joe. A clay pot among glittering silver vases. One lone man among the thousands and thousands of people in Athens. A foreigner and outsider in a cosmopolitan arena. (Paul's hometown of Tarsus was no backwater village, mind you, but in comparison to the intellectual mystique of Athens, it still may have felt small.)

We are practically blinded by the irony of these circumstances. For so many years Paul had tirelessly studied the Scriptures to arrive at truth, yet had missed the One to whom they all pointed: Jesus. Now he stood among the city touted for its intellectual advances and incessant pursuit of knowledge, and those within it had not yet heard the most important truth of all: the grace offered through Jesus Christ. Yet now Paul held within him the treasure of the gospel of Jesus Christ. And he knew he had to share it.

Read aloud Acts 17:16–17 and consider the following:
Describe Paul's emotional state.

What specifically made him feel that way?

What action did he take as a result?

What new location do we see Paul go with "his treasure" in this city?

Unlike the reports from the other cities Paul visits, we are not told how the Athenian Jews responded to the message. This visit speaks strictly of the Gentile response. Interestingly, Paul engages with two groups of people who held worldviews still widely espoused today. And yet we see similar responses to the gospel message.

Read aloud Acts 17:18–21.
Identify the two groups of philosophers Paul encounters and write them below.

How would you describe their initial response to Paul's message?

How do you think Paul felt at their suggestion to come present his ideas to the Areopagus?

> Briefly, the Epicureans held a theory according to which the world and the gods were a long way from one another, with little or no communication. The result was that one should get on with life as best one could, discovering how to gain maximum pleasure from a quiet, sedate existence. The Stoics, however, believed that divinity lay within the present world, and within each human being, so that this divine force, though hardly personal, could be discovered and harnessed. Good human living then (virtue) consisted in getting in touch with, and living according to, this inner divine rationality.[9]

We still see these two philosophies widely embraced today, do we not? The Epicureans relentlessly pursued pleasure, thinking little of eternal consequences or divine displeasure. Life is meant to be enjoyed and all this "religious stuff" interferes. In contrast, the Stoic resembles the modern-day humanist. Pleasure is not the highest pursuit, rather it is virtue, or as we often see today, knowledge or industriousness. A life that contributes to the greater good is the goal. That greater good can be economic prosperity, scientific discovery or advancement, excelling or creating in the arts . . . basically anything that is viewed as significant or elevating self to the highest state possible. Both of these philosophies stand in stark contrast to the Hebrew teaching of an intimate, personal God, who created us to know Him, directs our steps to good works to His glory, and has clearly identified our greatest purpose in life is to glorify His Son. No wonder they disputed with Paul!

While these philosophers may have enjoyed sitting around and discussing the latest ideas, they sneered at many of Paul's concepts. First of all, they suggested that Paul made no sense. He wasn't as intellectual as they were. The pursuit of knowledge was their highest aim. Knowledge of the universe allowed one to enjoy it more readily (Epicureanism), while for the Stoics, knowledge was indispensable to becoming virtuous. Second, they began to challenge his legal ability to be publicly proclaiming his message. Under Roman law, there was an approved list of gods to worship. The introduction of new gods could get you into some serious trouble. With rampant polytheism and many cults, groups of people would sometimes form secret societies in which they shared hidden beliefs. The philosophers' questions to Paul insinuates their suspicion that Paul may possibly be a member of one of them.

Thus, they challenged him to present his message in front of the Areopagus. This place (its Roman name is Mars Hill) at one time had been where the highest court in Greece met. By Paul's time, it was a meeting place where ideas of a variety of topics could be discussed and debated.

Write out Acts 17:21 below.
Can you relate this to something you see happening today?

Paul has the opportunity of a lifetime to preach to this influential crowd in the city of Athens. An audience totally unfamiliar to him, he needs to somehow create a point of entry, a connection to bridge the gap between his culture and theirs. How will he do it?

Tomorrow we will see how Paul expertly navigates this presentation, but in the meantime, let's pause for some reflection.

How does your heart respond when you see others pursuing modern day idols of pleasure, wealth, significance, or fame?

If you were put on the spot to defend your faith, have you considered what you might say? Take some time to write out some thoughts below:

This is the first time Paul is having to stand completely alone before a group of antagonists. Upon whom do you rely to stand strong in your faith when facing circumstantial or cultural opposition?

WEEK 5 | DAY 2
AN AREOPAGUS AUDIENCE
ACTS 17:22–34

We left off yesterday with Paul about to speak to the curious at the Areopagus. Today's reading offers practical and indispensable advice on how to share the gospel message with those who hold different worldviews than our own. While we first and foremost must know the contents of the gospel message, we must also think through how to deliver those contents on a practical level. This is what Paul teaches us today.

Write out below the gospel message in your own words. If you are not sure how to do this, seek the aid of a pastor or spiritual leader who can help you. You may also visit ericawiggenhorn.com for a basic gospel message.

Read aloud Acts 17:22–23.
Describe in your own words how Paul made a connection with the people of Athens. In other words, how did he affirm them?

How did he pique their curiosity regarding the message he was to share?

How did Paul play into the culture and interests of the philosophers by using this opening?

Read aloud Acts 17:24–25.

In what ways does Paul affirm Epicurean belief in these verses of Scripture? (Epicureans considered the gods to be so remote they took no interest, nor influence, in human affairs. The world was due to chance. There was no survival after death and no judgment.)[10]

Now read aloud Acts 17:26–27.

How does Paul explain Epicurean misunderstanding of this "unknown God"?

Before they are able to become offended by his suggestion that they have completely missed the boat in thinking that God is far off and uninvolved in their lives, Paul immediately circles back to another point of agreement. Isn't it interesting how people today "believe in God" yet feel as though He is far off and cannot be intimately known? Or they believe that He exists, but don't necessarily feel the need to earnestly seek Him out in their day to day lives?

In what ways do you see people today acknowledging God's existence but in many ways He is still unknown to them?

What does Paul cite as yet another commonality between them in Acts 17:28?

He is quoting the Athenian poet Aratus[11] and appealing to the Stoics who believe the gods can be known and are involved in the affairs of men. He is also appealing to the Epicurean idea that the world and the gods are indeed separate and disparate from one another. In other words, Paul intentionally makes an effort to connect with the philosophical beliefs of all members of his current audience.

Paul is equally piquing their curiosity as well as appealing to their common sense. In effect he is suggesting, "You are well versed in your philosophy about the world, yet logically you cannot deny there is a disconnect between the beliefs that you hold and evidence of its truth in the way people live their lives." So, Paul suggests an explanation for why this is so.

Read aloud Acts 17:29–34.
To what conclusion must one come regarding the gods?

What has now changed that requires a response (v. 30)?

How does Paul's statement in Acts 17:31 disagree with Epicurean philosophy? How does it appeal to the Stoics?

What specifically did the Athenians have a hard time accepting about Paul's message?

What was the result of Paul's message?

Let's revisit some of Paul's strategies a bit more closely.

1. He affirmed his audience and started with a point of agreement.
2. He understood the beliefs they held and the questions they had, and emphasized that our beliefs can and should affect how we choose to live.
3. He began with something that interested them.
4. He discussed an aspect of God's character (namely justice) that they found to be important if they were to believe in Him.

Look carefully over this list. How engaged do you think we need to be with cultural trends and ideas in order to share the gospel as Paul did here?

How well do you think you need to know a person in order to effectively address these issues in another person's life?

How do you see people expressing their desire to see some sort of cosmic justice today?

We may be called to share the gospel with a virtual stranger at times. We will probably be a lot more effective in sharing it with people we know, however. Taking the time to hear someone's heart long enough to be able to address their fears, answer their questions, and affirm them as a fellow human being in search of some answers about life and God would be pretty unexplainable in a world full of noise, now wouldn't it?

Visit ericawiggenhorn.com for Deeper Discoveries about Athens and Corinth.

GOD WILL GUARD HIS GOSPEL

ACTS 18:1–17

No doubt Paul had more to explain to the men of Athens regarding the "unknown god" they worshiped, but the mockery of resurrection by some of them led Paul to move on to Corinth. Unlike his other stops, there is no suggestion that he attempted to stay and strengthen the fledgling converts who had accepted the gospel message. Two of them, Dionysius and Damaris, are mentioned by name but are not ever mentioned again in Scripture. This whole story seems out of context from the rest of the narrative. We are not even told how the Jews of Athens responded. What is Luke's point in including it?

A couple of possibilities come to mind. So far on this second missionary journey, Paul has faced more obstacles than he has anything else. It wasn't until he received the call to go to Macedonia and he heeded it that he actually saw any response to the gospel. And that included three very unlikely candidates in Philippi (along with those of Lydia's household).

From there, also in Macedonia, Paul experienced acceptance of the message in both Thessalonica and Berea, albeit also tremendous opposition. Out of necessity, Paul is sent to Athens. God had not called Paul to preach there but due to incredible compunction in the face of so much idol worship, he could not contain himself. Yet, as far as we know, very little response to the message occurs. Could it be a lesson that no matter how eloquent our preaching may be, only the Spirit can draw hearts and reveal the truths of God? While Paul's techniques provide a lesson for us in sharing the gospel message with those who know little to nothing in the way of biblical truth, could the message for Paul be that unless God is the one leading him into the cities to preach, chances are he will witness little or no response to the message?

I also find it interesting that both Epicurean philosophy and Stoicism are widely prevalent thoughts in the Western world today. Could it be that God, in His infinite wisdom, sovereignly chose to include apologetic arguments against these world views, knowing that for centuries Christians would encounter people who held on to them? Several commentators actually criticize Paul's address to the Areopagus, claiming he failed to make a complete presentation of the gospel message. Yet we read that there were a handful of people who came to faith in Christ, so while Luke doesn't include all the details of Paul's message, I think it is safe to conclude that at some point he communicated all the gospel's elements to his audience.

What are your thoughts? Why do you suppose God sovereignly made sure to include this sermon in Athens on the pages of Scripture?

While the totality of all of sovereign wisdom behind this Athenian interlude remains hidden, Paul did not stay there; he traveled about sixty-five miles to the west to Corinth.

Read Acts 18:1–8 aloud.
Whom did Paul encounter in Corinth and why did he develop a relationship with them?

Why had this couple come to Corinth?

What did Paul do every Sabbath?

What happened when Silas and Timothy arrived?

Describe what happened between Paul and the Jews in Corinth.

Since Paul could no longer preach in the synagogue at Corinth, where did he now establish his ministry base?

Which Jewish man in particular believed Paul's message?

By the time Paul left Athens, he needed to earn money to provide for himself. The Greek word describing Paul's occupation as a "tentmaker" can also mean leather worker as well. Rabbis in Paul's day did not necessarily earn a living from their teaching the way pastors do today. In fact, all Jewish boys were taught a skill along with their knowledge received in rabbinic school. A Jewish proverb says, "Teach your son a skill or you teach him to become a thief." Paul frequently mentions in his letters that he chose to work to pay for his needs rather than exist off the gifts of the churches. However, once Silas and Timothy arrive, he apparently quits working and spends all day every day preaching, which implies that they had brought a financial gift along with them.

It is at this point that a disagreement erupts between the Jews of Corinth and Paul, and he is no longer welcome to teach in the synagogue. As a result, he begins teaching in the home of a Greek man, Titius Justus. He is described as being a worshiper of God. It is likely that he was not Jewish because, if so, it would have been assumed that he was a "worshiper of God." We see a great harvest of souls under Paul's ministry at Corinth. However, it appears that while Paul experienced that for which his heart yearned, he was also troubled.

Read aloud Acts 18:9–17 and answer the following:
What did the Lord say to Paul?

For how long did Paul remain in Corinth?

Of what did the Jewish leaders accuse Paul in front of the proconsul Gallio?

How did Gallio respond?

What happened to Sosthenes and how did Gallio respond to that incident?

Just when things started to heat up in Athens, Paul took off for Corinth. Now things are starting to get ugly in Corinth. Was Paul tempted to flee? I don't think God would tell Paul, "Do not be afraid," unless Paul was, well . . . afraid. God promises Paul that He will be with him and protect him, and we then read exactly how and through whom God kept that promise: Gallio. Interestingly, Gallio is not a believer, even though God told Paul that He had "many people in the city." I find this quite comforting and an incredible reminder that God is able to fulfill His plans and keep His promises through any and all people, not just those who call on His Name.

The ramifications of Gallio's edict cannot be overstated. While emperor worship was prolific in the Roman Empire by this time, the Jews were exempt from this requirement. Although Judaism forbade the worship of Roman gods, the Roman government considered Judaism a protected religion under Roman law and granted them freedom to practice monotheism. Gallio's response deeming Christianity to be a sect or part of Judaism set a precedent for its protection under Roman law. The Christians now had a pass to abstain from emperor worship as well. Despite this, we see Gallio's anti-Semitism in allowing the Greeks to beat Sosthenes without cause. God kept His promise to Paul and protected him. The gospel would remain unhindered within the province of Achaia and specifically the city of Corinth. The church in Corinth grew as Paul stayed on to teach there. And the church will continue on in our generation as well, as long as we keep on speaking and are not silent.

GOD WILL GUARD HIS GOSPEL CONTINUED

ACTS 18:18–28

Truly the ways of God are unexplainable. While Paul abruptly left Athens, without any clear explanation as to why, God divinely orchestrates events for Paul to remain in Corinth. His fears dispelled through a strange twist of events under the authority of Gallio, Paul settles in Corinth establishing the church. Thus far in his travels, this is the longest period that Paul stays in any one place. Certainly the church in Corinth needed and benefitted from Paul's extended presence. Composed of many displaced Jews from Rome, alongside Greeks coming out of a world of idolatry and licentiousness, this church needed a lot of direction. Much like the church in Antioch, many of its members held little to no knowledge of the Old Testament Scriptures upon believing in Jesus. They had much to learn. Finally, Paul found their faith effectively solidified to allow for his departure.

Read Acts 18:18–23 aloud.

Where did Paul sail and who accompanied him?

What did Paul do at Cenchreae?

What did Paul do in Ephesus?

Where did Paul's ship arrive?

What additional locations are listed in verses 22–23?

With these last couple of verses, Paul's second missionary journey is quickly wrapped up. However, there are some important details here that we don't want to miss. Paul, at some point, took a vow that involved not cutting his hair. Quite possibly it was a Nazirite vow, which one took in thanks for a blessing and/or as a sign of dedication toward God and Israel. (The Nazirite vow also included not drinking wine or touching anything dead for the duration of the vow; see Numbers 6.) Both purposes fit in Paul's life, since God had protected him in Corinth, and Paul may have made a vow of dedication to remain there in response to God's vision commanding him to stay. The one thing we can definitely take away is that Paul still revered many Jewish practices and did not abandon all traditions of Judaism. Though no longer judged by his adherence to them or lack thereof, he still found value and honored them as a Jewish man.

We are also given a bit of a prologue as to what is going to occur on Paul's third missionary journey, namely his long stay and miracles at Ephesus. To prepare for Paul's arrival into this dark city, God calls Priscilla and Aquila to go there first. These humble saints play a key role in the preparation for the gospel to arrive in this influential place. I can hardly wait to show this to you next week!

We also see Paul most likely heading to Jerusalem after disembarking at Caesarea since we are told he "went up" and greeted the church. This phrase was commonly used to describe the trek to Jerusalem since it was located in the hills. Since the Nazirite vow also involved taking one's sheared hair and bringing it to be burned on the altar, the story seems to weave its way through. It also would explain why Paul would have disembarked in Caesarea instead of directly in Antioch. Most important, we see Paul conclude this missionary journey by revisiting the churches he had established in Galatia and Phrygia. This gives us a glimpse into Paul's heart not only for evangelism, but also for discipleship. His desire was to see those who had accepted the message grow in their faith and stand firm in what they believed.

During Paul's return to Jerusalem, Antioch of Syria (his home church), and revisiting the regions of Galatia and Phrygia, something exciting is happening in Ephesus!

Read aloud Acts 18:24–28 and answer the following questions.
Who came to Ephesus while Paul was away and how is he described?

What did this man begin to do?

Where did this man go next and what was the result?

I love this little interlude so much. First of all, it tells us volumes about Priscilla's and Aquila's character. Essentially Apollos preached the baptism of repentance: preparation for the Messiah. He knew of Jesus, but did not know of His promise of the Holy Spirit. He did not know of the baptism that occurred at Pentecost, when the Holy Spirit was poured out upon believers. We learned that it was common for Jewish synagogues to allow guest speakers to come and share a word with the congregation. Since Apollos was a Jew visiting from Alexandria, he was welcomed to speak, and he began to preach about the Messiah. However, he had not yet heard the whole story of Jesus. Rather than cause a big fuss, Priscilla and Aquila invited Apollos into their home and shared with him the rest of the story.

What a beautiful picture for us to emulate. They didn't become angry with Apollos. They didn't criticize or gossip about his ignorance. They didn't raise concerns among the synagogue members as to Apollos's lack of understanding of the Scriptures. Instead, they welcomed him into their home and shared their lives along with the rest of the gospel story with him. I would love to see some more Christians out there like Priscilla and Aquila, wouldn't you? Hospitable, kind, and loving Christians, who take the time to explain the whole story rather than rant against those with whom they disagree.

While Apollos was a skilled rhetorician and highly knowledgeable of the Scriptures, he also appears to have a teachable spirit, receptive to further instruction.

Would you describe yourself as a teachable person? If so, in what ways? If not, in what ways do you feel you are not teachable?

We know Apollos was receptive to their instruction, because from there he went to Corinth with directions to the Corinthian church to welcome him openly. While there, Apollos continued to instruct this young church in the Scriptures. Paul had been led to disciple elsewhere, and God filled the gap through Apollos. How faithful He is to equip His saints! Unlike Paul, who admittedly came to Corinth in much fear and trembling, Apollos came boldly, speaking with eloquence. He was just the man to speak to Corinth's elite, who valued rhetoric and intellect. He was also able to refute the Jewish leaders due to his incredible knowledge of the Scriptures. A Jew himself, raised in the cosmopolitan city of Alexandria, he was able to help this church navigate the difficult unification of the displaced Jews from Rome with the Greeks from Corinth. God sent the perfect man to reach the culture and people of Corinth.

Consider Apollos's stop in Ephesus and his interaction with Priscilla and Aquila. If they had approached Apollos and his ignorance of the complete gospel message differently, what might have been the fallout? How did Apollos's interaction with Priscilla and Aquila equip him for this ministry assignment in Corinth?

While Priscilla and Aquila may have thought they were in Ephesus strictly to prepare the soil for Paul to return and sow the gospel seed, in reality they were there for multiple purposes, one of which was to disciple Apollos. In our fast-paced, transient culture we encounter many people for different seasons or maybe only a short while, as Priscilla and Aquila did Apollos. However, in every interaction, God is orchestrating and working. Will we be open to opportunities to invest in those whom God brings around us?

Can you identify someone in whom you see great potential, yet who may need some more maturity, knowledge, or discipleship? How could you come alongside them and help equip them for future kingdom work?

On the flip side, how do you intentionally pursue discipleship opportunities for yourself, to equip and prepare you for whatever God may call you to do?

THE HALL OF TYRANNUS

ACTS 19:1–10

Just a couple of weeks ago, I had the wonderful privilege of speaking at a camp in northern Arizona that hosts a women's retreat for churches from all over the southwestern United States. In two consecutive weekends, we had women from about forty different churches represented. We gave each church the opportunity to come up and tell one way they shared Jesus with the community in which they lived. The answers were astounding! Some offered tutoring to students, some fed the homeless, others visited nursing homes, hospitals, and jails. Some hosted moms' ministries, others provided job skills training. Basically, the ways these churches poured into their communities were as varied as the number of churches represented. It made me smile to think of God raising up people all over the southwestern United States to meet tangible needs and equip the body in such a variety of ways and places.

In this section of Acts, we have an interlude demonstrating how God did that in the early church. While Paul returned to his previously established churches, Apollos was raised up to further equip and establish the church at Corinth. Meanwhile, Priscilla and Aquila have remained in Ephesus in preparation for Paul's future arrival to preach the gospel there. In all these locations, God was working through different people and placed them in specific places to accomplish His purposes. This realization took me back to Paul's sermon in Acts 17:26–27 when he stated that God determined the exact time and place in which we should live.

For what purpose do you suppose God may have placed you within your church family?

In your community?

In your relationships (family, friends, and acquaintances)?

We are going to see today that Athens may have been the first time Paul took his message of Jesus out into the community, but it certainly wasn't the last. And as he did so, the message of the gospel exploded!

Read aloud Acts 19:1–9.
Who did Paul first encounter in Ephesus and what question did he ask them?

How did they answer?

What did Paul do as a result?

What happened when Paul laid hands on them?

These men resembled Apollos's understanding of the gospel. They had been baptized into a baptism of repentance, as had been offered by John the Baptist. They acknowledged their sinfulness and recognized their need for salvation, but as of yet, may not have heard of Jesus' arrival and fulfillment of salvation through His death and resurrection on the cross.

For how long did Paul speak in the synagogue in Ephesus?

This might be the longest stretch of time Paul has gotten to stay and speak any-where without trouble breaking out. While it's only conjecture, I have to wonder if Priscilla and Aquila had anything to do with that. They had been residents of Ephesus for a while now and no doubt worshiped in this synagogue. We have already learned what gracious souls they were by how they responded to Apollos. Could it be that due to their friendship with Paul, the Jews tolerated his zeal and tenacity for a longer period before blowing up at him? Or maybe Apollos had already gotten them thinking that Messiah had indeed come and now they needed to discover him for themselves. Paul purported to know how such knowledge was possible. Of course we cannot possibly know the answer to this, but it is good to remember that Paul did not preach in a vacuum. There were relationships and cul-tural events swirling around him that either aided or impeded his message, much like what occurs within the church today.

How does a pastor's good relationship with his congregation aid his teaching and other interaction with them? How could a poor relationship impede it?

What types of cultural events/philosophies make sharing the gospel more difficult? What might facilitate opening doors to share?

What happened after three months? Where did Paul go next?

How long did Paul "reason daily" at this location and, as a result, who got to hear his message?

As one of my pastors used to say: All means all and that's all all means. So when it says all the people heard the message, that's exactly what it means: all the people. It doesn't mean everybody believed it, but they all heard it. This is the first city in which we are told that all the people had a chance to hear the gospel. This is also the first city in which Paul began to preach and teach regularly within the community instead of strictly in the synagogue or someone's private residence. His teaching and preaching became much more accessible.

Ephesus was a great center for learning and housed the second largest library in the ancient world. Somewhere in the city's agora or marketplace area stood the hall of Tyrannus. Perhaps the space was used as a lecture hall in the cooler morning hours; Paul apparently rented it during the afternoon. As thousands flooded into the city of Ephesus daily for commercial and religious reasons, Paul's teaching of the Scriptures was daily conducted amidst the hustle and bustle of this thriving city.

Why do you suppose more people came to hear Paul's message in the hall of Tyrannus than they previously had at the various synagogues?

What are some creative places we could bring the gospel message that people would consider communal and on common ground?

What we saw in this week's homework is that God will guard His gospel. Whether the attacks come from other religions, governmental authorities, or those who have some knowledge of the truth but have failed to know or understand the full gospel, God will protect the message. He will raise up workers to deliver it and to gently instruct those who have not fully understood it. He will give His church the people they need in order to continue to grow. Despite opposition from many angles, the gospel will go forth in fullness and in power. He may ask us to take it to unexpected places, but if we could look around our community and assuredly say, "All the people in my community heard the Word of the Lord," that would be pretty unexplainable!

To where and to whom could you take the gospel?

unexplainable
RICHES

WEEK 6 | DAY 1
WHO ARE YOU?
ACTS 19:11–17

While Corinth was noted for its pleasure and sensuality, Ephesus heralded magic and sorcery. No wonder Paul spent so much time in these two cities. I'm sure it took months to break through longstanding spiritual strongholds. Throughout the Old Testament and during Jesus' ministry on earth, God manifested His power over false gods to demonstrate His sovereignty. God does the same thing in Ephesus through Paul.

How are Paul's miracles described?

What group of people began to attempt to use the name of Jesus like a magic formula without even believing in or understanding His Lordship? Why did they do this?

Who were some members of this group specifically?

How did the evil spirit respond to these men?

In this town of much sorcery, demonic activity proliferated. There seemed to be many people who suffered from demonic affliction in Ephesus, so much so that the town is filled with traveling exorcists. The darkness of Ephesus cannot be overstated. Interestingly, Ephesus was the most prosperous city in Asia Minor. Economic and social prosperity do not always equate to spiritual prosperity, just as economic and social poverty do not always mean those who live in such conditions are spiritually poor. In fact, some might suggest the opposite to be true!

The Jewish high priest resided in the city of Jerusalem presiding over the temple of God and the Jewish Sanhedrin. As did the chief priests. That Sceva, a chief or leading priest, would be residing in Ephesus means either he was head of the synagogue in that city or he assumed a sacred title that he indeed did not hold. The priesthood was a sacred calling and no one appointed himself into this role. I think his title may be an attempt to alert us to the use of Judaism as a status symbol rather than a true act of service as shepherd of the people of Israel who resided within Ephesus.

Regardless of how Sceva became assigned such a title, the evil spirits instantly recognized the absence of his sons' spiritual authority over them. Exorcisms were all in a day's work in the city of Ephesus, and traveling exorcists would come offering services of deliverance. Such was the work of Sceva's sons, however, that the evil spirit mocked them, saying he didn't recognize them. Then the man who had the evil spirit sorely beat these men, and they fled. In contrast, Paul's sweaty headbands and dusty aprons proved able to cure illnesses and afflictions presumed to be caused by the presence of demonic activity!

Often when I go walking, I encounter a certain small dog that runs after me and bites at my heels. It always appears out of nowhere and chases me from behind. The dog is not menacing per se, but its teeth are sharp and when it bites, it hurts! I finally discovered that when I turn around and face the dog directly, it instantly runs away. He is only brave enough to attack me when I am not looking and unprepared.

For those of us who have the Holy Spirit inside of us, we hold spiritual authority over the prince of darkness. He comes at times and from places where we least suspect him, but when we turn and face him, he will flee (see James 4:7). The truth is that he is more afraid of us than we ever should be of him. He can see the Holy Spirit within us and he trembles!

He also senses your giftedness, which the Holy Spirit desires to bring forth in your life. He cannot predict the future, but in reality he understands God's plans and purposes from a perspective that we sometimes do not. And so he deceives us into fearing him or beguiles us with things that look better than a life of following Jesus. But though his power is real, it is no match for the power of the Most High God who dwells within us!

Mark on the following scale how you generally respond to the idea of evil spirits/spiritual warfare:

I DON'T LIKE TALKING ABOUT THIS STUFF	I KNOW THEY EXIST BUT I DON'T OFTEN THINK ABOUT IT	I OFTEN AM AWARE OF SPIRITUAL WARFARE

Write out Ephesians 6:12:

Paul vividly understood that we have a real enemy and we are actively fighting against him. He equated it with war. He also intimates that victory is indeed possible, so long as we are prepared for the fight; our battle is won with Scripture and prayer.

In fact, while it may initially seem that the evil spirits won a battle over the seven sons of Sceva, in actuality, Paul's ministry won. Out of that incident, the name of Jesus was revered. The enemy's tactics will always come back to haunt him. His momentary display of his power led to the one thing he hates most—glory given to the name of Jesus.

How does Paul describe Jesus' authority over the powers of darkness in Ephesians 1:20–23?

If Christ lives in us, the hope of glory, how then should we respond to the powers of darkness around us?

Carefully read Ephesians 3:20–21.

Through what means does God work and display His power?

Pause for a moment and think of an area of your life where you are living in fear or striving to succeed in your own strength. Based on today's Scripture passages, what do you think the Holy Spirit may be prompting you to do?

AN IRREVOCABLE CONFESSION

ACTS 19:18–20

When I taught elementary school, the phenomena of guilt never ceased to amaze me. If one student got caught for disobeying in a particular area, it seemed that several others immediately needed to come and confess their crimes. One year some of my second graders decided they wanted to form secret clubs. The conditions for membership appeared rather fickle and arbitrary, and I began having student after student approach me in tears when they had suddenly been ousted. Since there were several different clubs, and membership remained elusive, I knew I needed to address it with the whole class.

I sat them down on the carpet and began to read *You Are Special* by Max Lucado. In the town of the Wemmicks, stars were assigned to good, successful Wemmicks and dots for those who do not shine in any particular way. One particular Wemmick, Punchinello, has never had a star in his life, only dots. One day he meets Lucia, a Wemmick without either stars or dots and he is mesmerized by her ability to be star and dot free. She shares with him her secret: Go see Eli the Wemmick maker. Once Punchinello goes to see the one who made him, he realizes that the stars and dots are meaningless.

I then took out packs of star stickers and dot stickers and showed them to the class. I asked, "Who can tell me what we could do in class that should earn us stars?" Their answers varied. "Be good listeners," "behave," "be kind to each other," and so on. Then I said, "Would you like me to also put a red dot on you every time you forget to do one of those things or behave in a certain way?" Their eyes got big and they all shook their heads no, emphatically disagreeing with that idea.

I then explained, "When we tell people they can be in our club, it's like putting a star on their shirt. When we tell them they can't, it's like placing a big red dot on their forehead. It's unkind. It also doesn't allow us to be like Lucia who felt confident in who she was made to be, without anyone else telling her so. The clubs need to stop. If you are in a club or have organized one, I want you to think about how you are making other people feel."

Within the next hour I had students coming to me in tears admitting what they had done. Others wrote notes of confession and put them on my desk or in my coat pocket. I saw others go and hug their friends and apologize. Once the cat was out of the bag, or the stickers out of the package, guilt spread like wildfire. So it is today with the Ephesian sorcerers.

Read Acts 19:18–20.
After the incident with the seven sons of Sceva, what did many believers do?

What else did they do, causing their commitment to end their practice of sorcery to become irrevocable?

What resulted from this act of obedience on the part of the Ephesian believers?

The cost of these scrolls totaled an estimated 50,000 days' wages. This was a huge sacrifice on the part of these believers. That which had notably been their most valuable and prized possessions became the very things they needed to destroy.

What are some of your most valuable and prized possessions? Have you irrevocably given them over to the Lord?

Our possessions may not need to be burned in order to be sacrificed, but this passage invites us to pause and examine our possessions. Do we view them as tools through which the Word of God might be spread? What about our homes? Our vehicles? Our bank accounts? Do we see them as opportunities for the power of the gospel to become magnified? How do we use them to bless people? Or meet needs with them?

This act of obedience on the part of the Ephesian believers illustrates the climax of what happened within Paul's two-year period of evangelism and discipleship here. In essence, those who chose to believe Paul's message and follow Christ gave up everything from their old life and began to embrace the new. As a result, the gospel spread widely and with power!

> For more on the cities of Ephesus and Colossae, see Deeper Discoveries at ericawiggenhorn.com.

Let's pause here and sit at the feet of Jesus. Allow Him to speak to you quietly within your heart. Is there anything in your life to which you are clutching tightly? Is there something He is asking you to let go of? Something or someone whom you need to place in His hands? Have you made an irrevocable commitment to follow Jesus no matter what the cost? Are you willing to make one now?

Record what He reveals to you below:

WEEK 6 | DAY 3
ONLY ONE MAN
ACTS 19:21–22

Something incredible is happening here that I don't want us to miss. Originally Paul preached in the synagogues. In his ministry at Corinth, he began preaching in a home. Now in Ephesus he is preaching in the public square. No wonder we are told that the Word of the Lord spread widely! Paul was open to delivering the message of Jesus in whatever venue the Lord allowed. We expect the gospel to be preached in our modern-day churches, but are we as apt to view alternative venues as possibilities for the gospel to be shared?

How often is the gospel expressly shared within your church?

How can we share the gospel within our homes?

How can we share the gospel in the public square?

Why do you think God had Paul preach the gospel in all three of these places?

Despite all this growth, Paul continued to look onward and outward to where God might call him to take the gospel next. In light of this explosion of growth, it quickly became apparent that Paul needed an army of pastors and disciplers to keep the churches going. He could not keep up with the work alone. Paul felt a heavy burden of responsibility for the churches he had planted (see 2 Corinthians 11:28). Yet, he also felt the call to take the gospel even farther west to the very edges of the Roman Empire (see Romans 15:24). How could he do both?

According to Acts 19:21–22, what were Paul's current travel plans?

Which two colaborers did Paul send ahead of him to revisit the churches in Macedonia?

Essentially Paul wanted to retrace his steps and revisit the churches he had planted thus far. This included the Galatian and Philippian churches. I love the heart Paul has for the believers everywhere he went. He didn't evangelize and move onward; his heart remained continually vested in the care and growth of the people with whom he had shared the message of Christ. These travel plans included hundreds of miles, so it was no small feat to retrace his steps like this. We also know part of his reasoning in doing so was to gather a collection to take to the impoverished church in Jerusalem (see Romans 15:25). Paul cared about their physical needs as readily as he did their spiritual growth.

To which aspects of Paul's ministry can you most relate? Do you prefer to look outward into the future and plan what God may have for you next, or do you prefer to look inward and equip those immediately around you?

Why is it important to do both?

Whom has God given you to be a colaborer in ministry? This could be someone who helps you in your role as a wife or mom, someone whom you regularly serve alongside of at church or in a parachurch ministry, or something else.

How do you see each of your gifts/passions complementing one another?

If you cannot identify a colaborer in ministry, begin to pray and ask God to send you someone. Also pray that God would mold you into a person who is willing to reciprocally invest in others. Paul could continue to travel and evangelize, but if there was no one to oversee the churches and continue to disciple them, it is quite possible the churches would disband and the believers' faith would fizzle.

Paul spent three years in the region of modern-day Turkey equipping and establishing the church of Ephesus. From there the gospel spread out to the world. Today fewer than one percent of the people of Turkey—or about 120,000 in a country of almost 80 million—consider themselves Christian. Turkey is nearly 98 percent Muslim. These brave followers of Jesus persevere in their faith though they are such a small minority. I had the opportunity to travel through this area last year with a group of people from our church. As we stopped at the ruins of each of these ancient churches, we prayed for the people of Turkey, that God would bring them another Paul to share the hope of Christ. As we interacted with the people of Turkey, I could see the fear in their eyes. I wished I could communicate with them, but I could only motion that I was praying for them, which brought tears to the eyes of some and smiles to the lips of others as I held up my gold cross to let them know it was to Jesus I was praying.

Picture the community in which you currently live. In another fifty years, do you believe your church will still be sharing the gospel? Why or why not?

What do you suppose God is calling you to do in your church in your generation to ensure the gospel will continue to stand?

If you are a person like me, who often holds back or feels reluctant to openly share your faith with others, pause here and pray for courage to be braver in sharing the hope of Christ on a daily basis.

WEEK 6 | DAY 4
GAINS AND LOSSES
ACTS 19:23–34

When Jonathan and I were first married, he worked in the late afternoons and into the evening. I hated coming home to an empty house after teaching school and often felt afraid. So we got a dog—a big, black pit bull–Labrador mix we rescued from the dog pound. She was my shadow and stayed within five inches of me whenever I was home. I have been a dog person ever since. Even now, when I spend most of my days at home studying and writing, my two dogs are by my side. And I still prefer not to be alone.

But often when I travel to speak or attend writers conferences, I go alone. When I'm alone, I have to battle my fear head on. This past summer in Cincinnati, nestled in my bed with my laptop, checking emails late into the night, suddenly my hotel room door swung open. Instantly I sprang to my feet charging the door like a wild bull shouting, "Get out, get out, get OUT!" as an identifiably intoxicated man staggered backward mumbling, "Isn't this my room?" "NO!" I shouted, slamming the door in his face and quickly swinging the safety lock across the door. I stood with my back against the door, every bone in my body shaking, trying to catch my breath. As I processed the event, the Lord spoke to me in the quietness of my heart. "My, look how far you've come in conquering your fear, child. Two years ago you would've sat paralyzed in your bed, too afraid to move. Well done!"

Today's event in Scripture records a similar experience in Paul's life. We assume Paul struggled with fear while at Corinth, since God spoke to him in a vision (Acts 18:9), promising to protect him while Paul preached within the city. When Paul was brought before the tribunal, God kept His promise without Paul even having to open his mouth to make a defense. In today's story, we read of another attack against Paul while in Ephesus. Yet this time around, Paul reacts boldly, without fear!

Read aloud Acts 19:21–34.

Who had left Ephesus?

Who served as the ringleader against Paul?

What was his primary concern?

How familiar do you believe he was with Paul's message? Why do you believe as you do?

How did he frame his greed to make it appear more noble?

How did Paul wish to react to these accusations?

Who convinced Paul not to venture into the theater?

Write down three adjectives to describe the crowd in the theater:

How did the Jews of Ephesus respond to this event?

I have stood in this theater at Ephesus. It holds close to 25,000 people. It is no small space by any means. This was mob mentality at its finest. No wonder most of those within it had no idea why they were there. They just jumped on the Artemis bandwagon. Demetrius the shrine maker would not have been the only craftsmen who benefitted from the worship of Artemis. (The Roman name for Artemis was Diana.) Her temple was larger than the Parthenon in Athens and stood as one of the seven wonders of the ancient world. People traveled from all over the empire to visit Ephesus and worship her. Innkeepers, food service providers, gift shop owners, various craftsmen, all benefitted from the worship of Artemis as tourists regularly flooded into town. And what happens to a town whose citizens rejected the main attraction? What would become of their city?

This gives us a clear picture of exactly what Luke meant when he said the Word of the Lord spread widely. There were not just a handful of people who rejected the Greek and Roman gods and the practice of sorcery, but there were enough people of the Way that business was affected. Livelihoods were at stake. Major revival was happening in Ephesus!

In the midst of the chaotic rage of the crowd, Paul desired to enter the scene. It quite possibly could have cost him his life, but all he could see was the size of the crowd and the opportunity to share the message of Christ. Paul reasonably listened to his friends, however—highly respected citizens of Ephesus, who persuaded him not to take such a risk. What a different Paul we see here. He desired to enter into an attack because of the widespread opportunity for evangelism. Not a fearful Paul. An energized Paul. While Paul appeared to have a bout of fear while in Corinth, he does not appear to struggle the least bit with fear in Ephesus; now he's ready to confront an angry mob of thousands with the message of grace. As someone who personally struggles with fear, this change in Paul's reaction brings me great hope.

What is a fear you battle against?

Have you seen God do a work in your life helping you conquer it? How so?

How might this fear prevent you from being most effective in the kingdom work God has for you?

If you could fast-forward two years, what would you hope to see change in your battle against this fear?

Even in a dynamo like Paul, God continued to peel back layers of his life he needed to surrender to God. Throughout that process, God afforded him many victories among the trials. And God desires to do the same with us. Step by step. Over time. In the midst of our faith journeys and our obedience, God is peeling back layers and giving us new areas of freedom and victory. So whatever you are facing today, don't give up! You may be cowering in a corner today, but charging like a wild bull tomorrow. And the change will be unexplainable apart from our wonder-working God!

WEEK 6 | DAY 5
GAINS AND LOSSES CONTINUED
ACTS 19:24–41

Standing on the streets of Barcelona, I felt certain I was going to be trampled to death. Suddenly out of nowhere, a mob of people began barreling down the street in full force. I froze in fear, unsure of what to do. The gates to the arena had opened and every man, woman, and child raced toward it hoping to secure a seat. The *futbol* game was about to begin (what we call *soccer*). Our Spanish teacher snatched us one by one, dragging us safely back into the café away from the rushing current of fans. "Barcelona! Barcelona!" they shouted as they made their way into the arena.

Unlike these wildly energetic soccer fans, most of the men and women in the theater at Ephesus had no idea why they were there. They just rallied around their prized goddess and civic pride. Nevertheless, the frenzy increased.

What a sad picture of the state of humanity apart from a Savior. People don't know why they are here or there or where they are going or why. They just blindly follow the crowd and listen to whoever is noisiest. Maybe they want to be part of the "in crowd," or they're curious or looking for excitement; then one day they suddenly wake up and wonder, "What *am I* doing here?" Or they never wake up at all and spend their entire life chasing the latest rush of fools. They just keep shouting and running, hoping to be heard and to find the satisfaction they're desiring.

I wonder if Paul recalled this event when he penned Romans 1:28. Write the verse here. What does he say in this verse about man's ability to reason and process truth?

I find it so interesting that it wasn't until someone in authority stood up and agreed with this frenzied mob that they finally settled down.

Read aloud Acts 19:35–41.

How does the city clerk agree with the views of this mob?

What two things does he claim Paul, Gaius, and Aristarchus are innocent of?

What does he suggest Demetrius and company should do instead of rioting?

What concerned the city clerk regarding this event?

How did the assembly respond to his concern?

I'm not sure exactly where the city clerk obtained his information about the origination of this mob, but one thing he said struck me as odd. He claimed that Paul and his companions had not blasphemed Artemis. Um, I'm pretty sure saying she wasn't actually a god at all would be considered blasphemous, would it not? Again, we see how utterly misinformed the vast majority of the people are who are standing in this crowd screaming their heads off.

Not only does he suggest that Paul and his companions had not in fact done anything wrong, he takes things a step further by insinuating that Demetrius and the craftsmen had behaved uncivilly. The city of Ephesus and the Roman govern-ment held proper channels to address grievances, and these men operated outside of the boundaries. Their behavior could get the city in serious trouble with Rome and possibly even cost them their freedom to govern themselves. You better believe that anyone who had an issue with Paul or his message was going to think twice before causing a riot over it. This was a sobering warning.

The freedom to preach the gospel had now been solidified in Corinth in the province of Achaia, and now in Ephesus in the province of Asia. While once again Paul faced intense opposition, through this event God eradicated barriers to share the message. Both governing authorities claimed the gospel of Christ and Chris-tian worship legally acceptable. Not only did this widely open doors for ministry, it undoubtedly brought Paul comfort knowing his churches were protected after his departure. Remember, Paul had set his sights on Rome. Yet again, the ene-my's attempts to thwart the gospel message and intimidate the early church only strengthened it. Paul and his message appeared unstoppable—the unexplainable church prevailed!

We would do well to pause and consider our own communities. Who stands to lose the most from the spread of the gospel within them? Stories are told that bars and taverns went out of business after the evangelist D. L. Moody came into town preaching. If revival happened in your city, whose livelihood would be at stake? Whose power would be questioned? Chances are these are the groups of people and places within our communities where we should focus our prayer efforts.

Who would be most opposed to the gospel in your neck of the woods? Why?

How might fervent, focused prayer for this particular organization or group of people help facilitate revival in your city or town?

I believe prior to this event, Paul felt uncertain if the Ephesian church could withstand his departure. Maybe he did not feel the people were effectively discipled enough to carry on in their faith. Maybe he still felt he had more work to do and more key leaders to train. Maybe he feared the great opposition the Ephesian believers faced within their city. We cannot know for sure, but Paul's correspondence to the believers in Corinth during this time sheds some light on his thinking.

Read 1 Corinthians 16:5–9.

Why did Paul consider it important to remain in Ephesus?

There will always be adversaries against our message. However, they cannot stop God from opening a door for effective ministry. Is God opening a door for you, friend? Don't be afraid to walk through it!

unexplainable
PROTECTION

WEEK 7 | DAY 1
MUCH ENCOURAGEMENT
ACTS 20:1–6

Rather than evangelizing new places, Paul now spends his time revisiting and strengthening already existing churches. Other than Rome, Paul will not personally establish any new church plants. Due to the historical events of this time period, the early believers need much strengthening and encouragement. The inclusion of many Gentiles into the Christian church, with little to no background in the Scriptures, further necessitated repeated equipping and instruction. When Paul sets his sights on Rome, he knows that he will most likely never return to Ephesus. The words we encounter from Paul in this next chapter are spoken by a man who knows this will be the last time he lays eyes on his listeners.

Put yourself in Paul's shoes for a moment. If you knew you were to spend your very last day with your family, what would you say?

What would you say to your church family?

According to Acts 20:1–2, what types of words did Paul choose to speak?

Using the map in the back of your study book, fill out the chart below:

PAUL'S CHURCHES IN MACEDONIA   PAUL'S CHURCHES IN GREECE (ACHAIA)

_____   _____
_____   _____
_____   _____
_____   _____
_____   _____
_____   _____
_____   _____

Knowing what you do about the churches located in Greece, why do you suppose Paul decided to remain there for such a lengthy time?

Read Acts 20:3–6.

For what reason was Paul unable to return to his home church in Syrian Antioch?

Why do you suppose Paul took men from so many different churches along with him as traveling companions?

If there is one word I would use to describe Paul, it would be *intentional*. He had well-thought-out reasons behind everything he did—everything. He was a man of prayer and purpose: what may appear on the pages of Scripture as madness in his roundabout travels actually had been highly directed by the Holy Spirit. Not only was he intentional regarding his travels, he was purposeful in whom he invited to accompany him. Paul not only taught, he mentored. He invested in men to whom he would one day pass the baton of the churches and he chose them carefully.

Think of Luke. He traveled with Paul for the purpose of constructing a historical account of what occurred after Jesus' resurrection and ascension. An excellent scribe, Luke could be trusted to faithfully record that which Paul deemed necessary to be recorded long after he had departed. These stories, lessons, and commands needed to be immortalized in ink to ensure the continued equipping of the church. But Paul knew the church needed more than just his written words—it also needed leaders.

Paul recognized in Timothy pastoral and leadership gifts, and poured into him diligently to oversee the churches. There were others as well, because Paul often mentions their names at the end of his letters.

He also sought a level of transparency in his ministry. Having someone from each of the churches who was known and respected by their members accompany Paul meant that the leaders could return to their own faith families and vouch firsthand that Paul indeed lived out on a daily basis the message that he preached. No doubt these men needed to hold spotless reputations themselves in order for the veracity of their reports to be taken seriously. Otherwise their word spoken on Paul's behalf would not hold any weight.

Paul and his companions also carried a large collection of money they had collected from the various Gentile churches to deliver to their Jerusalem brothers who currently were suffering from a famine in Judea.[12] While a large group not only afforded safety, this collection of men also demonstrated the solidarity sought among the various Gentile churches and their Jewish brethren in Jerusalem.

Paul sought men who could equip, lead, and authenticate his message and his mission. So he chose his entourage carefully to fulfill that purpose. Imagine if Paul were standing in your church choosing his traveling companions and his eyes rested on you.

What character traits, skills, talents, and gifts would Paul see that could be used to equip the church?

What are some areas where you could step up and take a greater role or responsibility?

What kind of reputation do you hold within your faith family? What are some practical things we must do/not do to be known as people of our word?

We often get so wrapped up in being a type of leader within our culture. I love that Paul didn't only invest in those in whom he saw the gift of leadership. I believe as I do because often when Paul refers to his fellow laborers at the end of his letters, he cites their faithful service and strong character rather than their leadership skills. He also chose to invest in those who were simply deemed genuine and faithful. They were just as important to Paul and his ministry as everyone else. Maybe Paul learned this lesson the hard way after writing off John Mark and later seeing this young man emerge as an indispensable member who regularly offered pastoral care to the young churches.

Read 3 John 5–8 and record how a man named Gaius (not the same individual named in Acts 20) is described:

A faithful follower who opened his home to traveling disciples. No fanfare. Not a big leadership role, just simple and genuine hospitality. John reminds Gaius that the one who furnishes the meal and/or the bed is a fellow worker in the spread of the gospel. In other words, equally important.

Do you view all service done for the kingdom as equally important? Why or why not?

Why do you think people sometimes feel like they have to do big things for God in order for their service to count?

The message in today's reading is a reminder to live intentionally. It is also a reminder that our character is equally as important as our actions. To be described as faithful, genuine, and loving might be the most unexplainable accomplishment there could be.

Pause here for a moment and allow the Holy Spirit to speak to your heart. What do you sense Him saying to you today?

WEEK 7 | DAY 2
A LIFE RAISED FROM SIN AND DEATH
ACTS 20:7–16

As we make our way through this chapter we are going to witness over and over again a long list of last words and good-byes. It blesses me greatly knowing what I do about the church at Philippi that Paul chose to spend Passover with them (20:6). Of all the churches with whom he would spend this sacred holiday, it was the place where he finally understood God's incredible grace. I also love that Paul made sure to spend a longer time in Greece as he knew of the struggles that occurred within the Corinthian church. Again, we see Paul being so wonderfully intentional and relational in his timing.

Why did Paul talk so long at Troas?

Since Eutychus had to sit in the window sill, what can we presume about the size of the crowd crammed into this house?

Undoubtedly, not one single person in that room at Troas would forget the miracle they witnessed that night!

After this miraculous night, Paul separates from the group and travels to Assos on foot, presumably alone.

Why do you suppose after all these good-byes and performing this mighty miracle, Paul would choose to spend a couple of days alone?

Under what types of circumstances do you feel the need to spend some time alone?

According to verse 16, what decision did Paul make at this time?

Within these few short verses Paul experienced tremendous highs and lows emotionally. He said good-bye to some of his dearest friends. He also was used by God to perform an incredible miracle. He had much to process. What we see, however, is that Paul has a plan. He has a goal in sight that he is pursuing relentlessly. He will not be distracted or dissuaded. Often we need to pull ourselves away and make sure we have our sights set on the right things.

What does the writer of Hebrews exhort us to do in Hebrews 12:1–2?

Pentecost occurs fifty days after the Feast of Unleavened Bread, also known as the Passover. It has been at least seventeen days since Passover, and Paul has a long voyage to reach Jerusalem. We do not know Paul's exact reasoning for wanting to be in Jerusalem on this holiday, especially since we are told that the Jews have been plotting to kill him. Since he was delivering a sizable benevolent collection for the Jewish Christians, it may be he wanted it delivered when it would have the most impact, since many Jews would be present for the pilgrimage feast. From all that we know of Paul by now, however, we can assume he has a very specific reason for wanting to be there.

Knowing what you do about Paul's time in Ephesus, why do you suppose he decided not to reenter it to say good-bye to the believers there?

Why do you think Paul may have desired to be in Jerusalem on Pentecost?

In case you haven't picked up on it yet, I sense a great climax brewing in Paul's ministry. A major shift of events is about to unfold, and his role as a traveling missionary is coming to a close. A new era in his ministry is about to begin. Based on Paul's actions, we can infer that he knew it as well and adjusted his plans accordingly. The pace of the narrative quickens substantially and we see Paul hopping from place to place quite quickly in preparation for this next season of ministry.

How would you describe your own season of ministry at this point in your life? Are you in the preparation stage as Paul was in Antioch? Are you in the development stage as Paul was on his first and second missionary journeys, growing and learning all the time? Are you settled in a particular place for a stretch of time as Paul was in Ephesus, witnessing a harvest for your faithfulness and obedience? Or are you in a time of preparing for a great shift as Paul is now?

Pause here for a moment and describe your own journey of faith and service below:
What do you sense the Lord is saying to you in this season of your life?

Do you feel as though your spiritual journey is speeding up or slowing down? In what way(s)?

How are you being intentional in this season?

What emotions are you experiencing?

Honestly, I think this leg of Paul's third missionary journey may have been his most difficult. I think he instinctively knew it was time to let go of his leadership of his beloved churches. God was moving him on to something else. He would never see them again. We know from his letters how deeply he loved these men and women. He agonized in prayer over them. He rejoiced at their growth. He wept when they got off track. And he had to let them go. I imagine I might be able to relate to Paul's feelings more readily when my children go off to college or get married. While Paul knew they were in God's hands and he had done every-thing he could to prepare them, it still must have broken his heart. And yet, he obeyed. He loved them with his entire being, yet held them with open hands, knowing they had been entrusted to him for a season.

We too have been entrusted with families, friendships, and ministries for such a time as this. Are we loving them with everything we have, yet holding them with open hands? Are we being intentional with the time that we have? We all have a role to play in the unexplainable church!

WEEK 7 | DAY 3
THE PURITY OF THE MESSAGE
ACTS 20:17–27

During our initial exploration into the adoption process, I spent hours researching. There were so many different agencies. Should we adopt domestically or internationally? Which agencies specialized in which types of adoption? How do we start our home study? I had an endless list of questions, and while the answers were out there somewhere, they seemed buried in a labyrinth of horror stories and cautionary tales. The process felt overwhelming and exhausting.

In the midst of all of it I came across Shaohannah's Hope, now called Show Hope, an organization started by Christian singer/songwriter Steven Curtis Chapman. He and his wife, Mary Beth, had adopted two little girls from China and sought to use their platform to aid other families in the adoption process. I had the opportunity to hear Steven speak about his own family's adoption process and why adoption was so dear to their hearts.

Since that experience of sitting across the table from him and listening to him tell his own faith journey, adoption story, and walk with God in the midst of it, I have never heard his songs quite the same. Rather than just hearing the lyrics, I connect with the heart of the one singing them. I sense the passion from which they were written. I know the man's story behind his songs. And the words came to have greater impact. I don't know Steven personally. I don't know all the ins and outs behind why he chose to write all the lyrics he did in his hundreds of songs, but I do feel like I know his heart.

I know he loves Jesus passionately and wants to serve Him with every ounce of his being. I know he strives to live in obedience to the leading of the Spirit in his life. I know he wants to finish the race marked out for him and hear, "Well done." This much I know.

That is how I feel when I read Paul's farewell address to the Ephesian elders today. After spending so much time walking alongside him through his letters, marking his endless travels on a map, and listening to his prayers for the churches, I feel as though I know his heart. And these words spoken to these men in today's passage pierced me deeply.

What three things did Paul assert the Ephesian elders knew about him? Circle them below:

How he lived (that his life matched his message)

What he ate for breakfast

That he served the Lord in faithfulness and humility

How much he hated writing letters

That he faithfully preached the full truth of God's Word

Did Paul declare there was any difference in his message to the Jews and the Greeks?

What did Paul know in regard to the future? What did he not yet know?

Write out Acts 20:24 below:

For what reason did Paul insist that they all hear this message from him at this moment?

Finish verse 27: For I _____

_____.

I recently received a text message from a friend of mine asking for prayer. She writes a daily blog, and someone contacted her asking to be removed from her list of subscribers. The reader complained that she wrote too many things that she found to be offensive and suggested that she return to only writing about encouraging topics while steering away from controversial ones. My friend was devastated and struggled with this admonishment from one of her readers. When she asked my advice, I suggested that if she never said anything that some may find difficult or disagreeable, chances are she wouldn't be writing much of substance. My counsel was that she prayerfully examine her purpose in blogging and go from there.

Paul knew he had to teach the full counsel of the Word of God. Even the parts that were going to rub some hearers the wrong way. Sections that would make people upset. Yet Paul knew that to only preach and teach the parts that would be well received would not be helpful and God would hold him responsible. He wanted these elders to know that he was leaving them with a clear conscience. He had been willing to preach the difficult portions of Scripture as readily as those everyone would go home and feel good after hearing. The elders needed to follow his example in this.

Paul references Ezekiel's prophecy twice in this short departure sermon.

Read Ezekiel 33:7–11. How had Paul's messages to the churches alleviated him from accountability for the rebellion of his hearers?

According to Ezekiel 34:1–10, what does God expect of His shepherds?

More and more I see churches skirting difficult issues. Cultural pressure causes us to sweep things under the rug as if we could somehow cover up an elephant. We cease to confront sin. We cave to the lie that calling out sinful behavior is judgmental. We justify our failure to do so because we are well aware of our own sinfulness and our failure to begin to intentionally root it out of our lives. So we stick with comfortable topics like grace and glory. We talk about God's love and acceptance. We've shrunk God's grace to a white flag of acceptance of our sinfulness rather than an unexplainable power to help us overcome it. We have defined God's love as a willingness to look away from our sin and pretend it's not there instead of an unexplainable presence that brings our sin out into the glorious light yet without condemnation. We've claimed that our sinfulness is really just too big to overcome in this life, so why even try?

Today in the church a dangerous theology is developing. It suggests that there are some sins that God's grace cannot overpower. We must therefore accept those who struggle with them without question, the assumption goes. To suggest otherwise—such as that believers hold Christ's power within them to overcome all sin—must be unkind, judgmental, unfair. Their sin is greater than God's grace, so they have no choice but to succumb to it, and a misguided theology of grace tells us we should accept that.

So we stick the tough stuff in a box and shove it in a corner. But the corner is getting awfully full, and it's only a matter of time before all those issues we've stacked up are going to come crashing down like an avalanche upon us. Because

God never intended for us to simply shove hard things aside and pretend they're not there. He intends to remove it—all our sin—as far as the east is from the west (Psalm 103:12). He intends to fill us with His unexplainable power and begin a journey toward greater and greater freedom as His Spirit fills us with love, joy, peace, patience, kindness, goodness, gentleness, and self-control. It's not perfection we will achieve in this life but neither is it hopeless degradation. Paul clearly taught that within the life of the believer there was a standard of morality to which one was expected to strive. While struggle with sin is to be expected, surrender to sin with no aim of trying to overcome it is unacceptable.

Grace was not only given to cleanse us from sin; it was also given to empower us to be released from its grip on our flesh, hearts, and minds.

What are some controversial topics within the "whole counsel of God" that you see the church preferring to avoid?

How have you seen people use the doctrine of grace as justification for sin?

How have you seen people minimize grace as an acceptance of sin rather than a powerful plan of God to help the believer overcome it?

The truth is that Jesus taught some hard things. Think of it this way: He didn't tell us to pick up a twig. He told us to carry a cross.

Does this concept alarm you? Encourage you? Challenge you?

Paul didn't claim that to fellowship with Christ may involve only disappointments and frustrations, but that He called us to join Him in His sufferings. Christ doesn't ask us to follow Him only when the path is easy and predictable; He calls us to bind ourselves to His mission even in the dark, the difficult, and the dreadful. Because this world is not our home. The glory is coming. Complete freedom and perfection is not in this life, it's in the life to come. But Jesus tells us to take heart, because He has overcome the world. And this means with Him we can do hard things, and do them well.

This means we can wrestle with difficult portions of Scripture. This means we can admit we don't live perfect lives, but we can still boldly maintain that some things are sinful. This means we can confess that we struggle to aim for godliness and often miss the mark, but we never cease trying, because we have one who is interceding for us in the battle and fills us with His Spirit when the road gets long and we become weary. This means we will never settle for the status quo spiritually; we will always strive for more, knowing with confidence that He who began a good work within us will be faithful to complete it.

Before you close your book today, spend some time at the feet of your Savior allowing Him to reveal to you any boxes you need to open and lay before Him.

WEEK 7 | DAY 4
GUARD THE FLOCK
ACTS 20:28–31

This past weekend I attended the annual fundraiser for the Choices Pregnancy Centers of Greater Phoenix. The keynote speaker admonished Christians to stop criticizing politicians for failing to publicly and unabashedly take pro-life and pro-family positions unless we as citizens were willing to do so ourselves. His point was that the churches should be as equally loud a voice for the sanctity of life and the biblical definition of marriage in the public arena as a politician should. As the old adage goes, "Don't preach what ya don't live." Don't harp on others to be vocal about issues if you're not willing to be so yourself.

Paul takes this same approach with the Ephesian elders. After Paul communicated his responsibility to the churches, he now shifted to theirs.

Write out the first five words of Acts 20:28:

The truth is that we cannot preach what we aren't willing to live. We cannot call others to a standard of morality for which we cease to strive ourselves by the power of the Holy Spirit. Any ministry or impact we make within the kingdom is going to come first and foremost out of the overflow of our relationship with Christ. He is the source of our power and we must regularly abide under His care.

According to Paul, who had made them overseers of the church?

To what vocation did Paul equate these elders?

From where would wolves come against the flock?

Based on Paul's warnings, how certain do you think he was of this happening?

Read 1 John 2:18–28.
Circle where John tells us to abide/remain in Christ.

Some of the distortions of the truth that the early church faced included the idea that Jesus did not actually have a bodily resurrection. Others claimed that He was an important prophet but not actually God's Son and equal with the Father. Some added Jesus into their pantheon of pagan practices as yet another addition rather than solely as the one true God.

According to Revelation 2:1–3, how well did these elders shepherd their flock against false teachers?

What did they fail to do, however? See verse 4.

It is important to note that the leaders of this church were firm in their teaching of sound doctrine. Scripture doesn't tell us why this second-generation church in Ephesus is described as having abandoned the love (for Christ) it had at first. But sometimes we pursue knowledge to the point of focusing on the mind more than on the heart.

In what ways do you see people emphasizing the truth of the gospel today in ways that may appear unloving?

How do you see an overemphasis on love without an emphasis on truth resulting in a distortion of the gospel?

How is Jesus described in John 1:14?

I have heard the way of grace and truth is a path between two guardrails: grace on the left and truth on the right. Most of the time as we travel the path we end up colliding sharply into one guardrail or the other, continually striving to steer ourselves securely into the middle, yet rarely able to do so. Too far in either direction and we get burned and scraped. And yet we follow in the footsteps of our Savior, who is the perfect blend of both of them.

Toward which guardrail do you generally tend to lean: grace or truth? How so?

What are some practical steps we as the church can and should take to strive toward a secure path between both of them?

One of the things I believe we as the church will need to do more and more in the days ahead is to stop being afraid to wrestle with difficult issues. We need to learn to be more comfortable with disagreeing and debating with one another in a respectful and productive atmosphere—not to prove one another wrong, but to sharpen one another. If our thinking is challenged and yet still stands, would we not feel more confident in our conclusions? We must be driven to the Scripture in an endless pursuit to solidify and clarify our thinking so we are always ready to defend our positions with gentleness and respect. Cultivating a culture in which we are diligently searching for greater understanding of God's Word, character, and plans for His people would probably result in fewer people jumping guardrails and abandoning essential doctrine. Instead, we develop our doctrine from our personal experience or bite-sized instruction from a tweet or Instagram meme, rather than going to the original Author who is able to guide us into all truth. We search for someone who agrees with our point of view more diligently than we search the Scriptures. If we were gracious enough to realize we still had things to learn yet truthful enough to disagree respectfully, wouldn't that be pretty unexplainable?

To learn more about the church at Ephesus later in history, see Deeper Discoveries at ericawiggenhorn.com.

WEEK 7 | DAY 5
COMMENDED TO GOD
ACTS 20:32–38

The last five years I lived in Michigan, three of my sisters in Christ and I formed the Bravo Team. The third Thursday of each month we met at a restaurant in Rochester Hills and encouraged one another. We prayed together, spoke Scripture over one another, and wrestled through major life changes from birth to death and everything in between. I remember the last time we met before two of us were to move away. We lingered on the patio long after the doors of the restaurant had closed. It was the end of a beautiful season of friendship. I cried the whole way home. I loved these girls so deeply and they had been so instrumental in my life during some of my darkest hours. Even to this day, over ten years and thousands of miles later, when a crisis hits, I know I can always count on their prayer support.

Have you ever had to say good-bye to someone whom you dearly loved? Describe the circumstances and how you felt:

I can only imagine Paul felt similarly about these Ephesian elders. For over three years he had taught these men, equipping them, leading to church plants through-out Asia Minor. Paul's life became so intertwined with theirs it would be difficult to imagine getting along without one another. No wonder they wept at his depar-ture. Their beloved teacher and friend would never return.

It's no wonder then why Paul needed to remind them, and no doubt himself, that he was entrusting them into the care of our glorious triune God. Paul brings in all three members of the Trinity when he says his good-byes to these elders at Ephesus.

Look back again at Acts 20:28 and record who appointed these elders as overseers:

Who purchased the flock?

Now look at Acts 20:32, and record which member of the Trinity is mentioned:

Write out Acts 20:32 below:

Underline what grace empowers us to do in this verse.

Why would it be important for these elders to remember that all three members of the Trinity worked together for the building up of the church?

Paul had taught and served alongside these men day in and day out for the past three to three-and-a-half years. He knew them intimately. He had lived and worked among them. They knew all that Paul taught and they had watched how he lived. Paul had not used his ministry as a means for financial gain or social popularity. He had taught and preached from a pure heart. He wanted to be remembered as a man who gave all of himself, not just his knowledge.

Paul also entreated them to cling to the Word of God after his departure. Through the word of grace they would continue to grow and be built up. No longer could they attend Paul's teaching in the hall of Tyrannus and elsewhere, but they could study the Word themselves. They could cling to his teaching and immerse themselves in it. Think of all that Paul had taught them over the last three years or so: over a hundred years of sermons crammed into thirty plus months. Yet Paul still entreated them to commit themselves to studying the Word.

So many Christians today are still young and weak in their faith. Truthfully, I consider myself one of them. It seems the more I study Scripture, the more I realize how much I have yet to learn. I feel as though it will take an entire lifetime to uncover all its treasures. We all can yet be further built up by the word of grace. And at such a time in our church history when so many resources are available for our growth—podcasts, books, Bible studies, videos, and more—week after week passes and too many of us feed on only a thirty-minute sermon delivered on Sunday morning. How many sermons would it take before a hearer could be confident they had received the full counsel of God's Word?

What practices, daily habits, and resources do you draw on to ensure you are being taught the full counsel of God's Word?

What impact could it have on the church if more Christians were committed to being built up by the Word?

What changes are you sensing you may need to make to help solidify your commitment?

While Paul entreats them to commit themselves to studying the Scriptures and immersing themselves in truth, he also exhorts them to care for one another as brothers and sisters in Christ. He quotes Jesus saying, "It is more blessed to give than to receive." While there is no record of this quotation of Jesus in the Gospels, Jesus frequently admonished His disciples against receiving payment for any miracles they worked in His name (see Luke chaps. 6 and 9 and Matthew 10). So when and where did Jesus specifically make this statement?

What is one possible answer to this question according to John 21:25?

How have you experienced the truth of the statement "it is more blessed to give than to receive" in your own life?

Unlike so many other traveling teachers and sophists, Paul refused payment for his ministry of teaching and preaching. Again we see Paul readily practicing in his own life that which he preached. When he came to the churches, he came to give, not to receive. Now he was calling them to give of themselves to one another and the work of the gospel in the same way Paul had given of himself to them. (Note that Paul is not suggesting those in ministry should not be paid; see 1 Timothy 5:17–18.)

How did Paul describe his ministry in 2 Corinthians 2:17?

To whom could you give of yourself today? Spend a few minutes journaling your thoughts below:

our
unexplainable
GOD

MORE GOOD-BYES
ACTS 21:1–6

The huddle of people along the seashore clung together at the end of our last session. The group wept at the thought that Paul was leaving and they would not see him again. But it was time for him to move on and minister to other churches and disciples.

The word used for "parted" in verse 1 is apospao, which means "to tear away." How does this word help us understand the emotion of the farewell?

Using the map at the back of your book, find and list below the places Paul and his companions traveled on the next leg of the journey in verses 1–6.

Where did they stay for seven days? What did the disciples there tell Paul in verse 4?

Upon what course of action did some of the believers present possibly disagree with Paul?

The believers in Tyre gave Paul a message "through the Spirit." Some commentators suggest that Paul, in his determination to go to Jerusalem, ignored the Spirit's word. Others maintain that "through the Spirit" meant these believers knew what Paul would face in Jerusalem, as we'll see later. These scholars' belief is not that the Spirit was telling Paul not to go, but that the believers' plea was out of their love for him rather than part of the Spirit's prophetic message.[13] Admittedly, it is a difficult verse.

It is interesting to note that in the midst of praying together, not all the believers reached the same conclusion as to how Paul should proceed with his travel plans. I think there is a lesson for us here. We are going to experience times of disagreement, situations in which we would choose to do things differently than another fellow believer. Neither one of us may necessarily be right or wrong, we just choose to proceed differently in obeying what we feel God is calling us to do.

Picture this beautiful scene: every man, woman, and child knelt together before God in submission to His will. Of course, this scene stands in stark contrast to what Paul's Gentile entourage will encounter when they reach Jerusalem's walls. At that point the men and women will be separated within the temple and they themselves will be even further relegated to keep their distance. This precious group of Tyrian believers painted a picture of Paul's heart for his churches.

How does Paul describe all believers in Colossians 3:11?

When we sense division among us and we fail to understand the heart behind another's speech or actions, what does Jesus tell us in Luke 16:15?

What does Peter assert in Acts 15:8?

According to Paul in Romans 8:27, how can we understand or intercede for the purity of others' hearts?

Is there someone you need to pray for today? If we never opened our mouths or our phones or tablets to share our opinion until after we had taken it to the throne in prayer, wouldn't that be pretty unexplainable?

WEEK 8 | DAY 2
THE WILL OF GOD
ACTS 21:7–16

I wonder if Paul and Philip met prior to the moment Paul knocked on his door. Paul: who heartily approved of Stephen's murder. Stephen and Philip served together as deacons in the Jerusalem church. Together they had been selected by Peter and the rest of the apostles as two of the seven men chosen to administer the resources of the church in caring for the widows and the poor. Had Philip ever laid eyes on Paul before? Was it through Philip that Luke was told the story of Stephen's stoning or had it been through Paul? What interesting dinner conversations must have occurred during Paul's stay! Can you imagine sitting across the table from someone who had cheered on the murder of your dear friend? Many years had passed since Stephen's death and both men had undoubtedly grown in grace and forgiveness.

What other guest arrives during Paul's stay at Philip's home?

What prophecy did he make concerning Paul's future?

How did Paul's traveling companions respond to this prophecy?

How did Paul respond?

To what conclusion did Paul's traveling companions eventually concede?

Have you ever had someone make a decision out of obedience to the Lord that was difficult for you to accept, or even broke your heart?

Why was it important for all the disciples to understand and believe that whatever happened to Paul, it was the Lord's will?

The unfolding of the Lord's plans can result in temporary hardships. Can you think of times when this has been the case?

What arguments do you think these men may have presented to Paul to try to convince him not to go?

For what reasons do you suppose Paul was so insistent on going to Jerusalem? You might want to refer to Acts 9:15–16; 19:21; 20:22–24; Romans 15:25.

If the Lord took Paul away from them, the disciples needed to rest in the belief that God deemed them ready to step up and fulfill the new mantle of leadership to which they would be called. Remember, those traveling with Paul to deliver the collection to the church at Jerusalem were notably men of strong character who exhibited leadership within the various Gentile churches. Also, in God's mercy, they were being given the opportunity to ask Paul anything they still felt they needed to learn or settle any questions that still lingered in their hearts.

Can you look back on a time in your life when you realized later that God was preparing you for something that was going to happen in the future?

The distance from Philip's home in Caesarea to Jerusalem is seventy miles. It required preparation, and some of the disciples from Caesarea accompanied them on their journey, no doubt providing animals and such to carry their provisions. In both Philip's and Mnason's homes we see the solidarity of the Jewish and Gentile believers as well as the inclusion of women into the tapestry of the church. For both of these Jewish men to invite these Gentile believers from the Greek and Asian churches into their home, they chose grace over the law. The Mosaic Law taught that inviting Gentiles into your home made it unclean. We see Philip's daughters honored with the spiritual gift of prophecy and the Tyrian women allowed to pray alongside the men at the beach prior to Paul's departure. These gracious pictures of unity will soon be starkly contrasted within the walls of the temple.

Are not these two gifts of God so often woven together in the fabric of life: grace and admonition? These Gentile believers accompanying Paul are repeatedly experiencing the beautiful grace of the unity of the church along with the warning and admonition of what is to come, not only through the words of Paul, but also the prophecies of Agabus along with the witness of the Holy Spirit Himself. And as the Unexplainable Church marches forward until the return of our King, may our eyes be wide open at the wonder of grace, and hearts be laid bare to receive His admonition and heed His warnings. May the Lord's will be done!

What do you need to give up and lay at His feet today?

PURPOSEFUL PURIFICATION

ACTS 21:17–26

wonder what went through Paul's mind as he made the seventy-mile trek from Caesarea to Jerusalem. He had heard Agabus's prophecy that the Jews would turn against him. Despite the danger, he pressed on, determined to deliver the offering that had been collected to the Jewish Christians in Jerusalem.

How much does Paul love his Jewish kinsmen, according to Romans 9:2–4?

How was Paul greeted by the Jewish Christians in Acts 21:17?

What did Paul tell James and the elders about the next day? See verses 18–19.

Oh, how I love the purity of Paul's heart. "Listen, James and my brothers, to what *God* has done!" How often I hear, "So many people are coming to Christ under so and so." "You wouldn't believe the work that *this church* is accomplishing." "The ministry under Pastor X is exploding."

Wrong, wrong, and wrong. God leads hearts to repentance. God does the work. The Holy Spirit expands and blesses ministry. People are merely tools. Objects placed in the hands of an always working, expertly planning, graciously expanding, unexplainable God. Apart from Him the object lies dormant and does nothing. In Paul's mind, he had done nothing. God had done it all. He was merely the tool in God's hands. And Paul was willing to be any type of tool to accomplish any kind of work to which God might call him.

How did James and the elders respond to this news?

Some misconceptions over Paul's teachings were circulating among some of the Jews. What were they?

What solution did James and the elders come up with?

How did Paul respond to their idea?

How does Paul describe his willingness to be flexible in 1 Corinthians 9:19–23 in order for as many to come to Christ as possible?

And in this passage Paul is willing to place himself under Jewish tradition in order to facilitate reconciliation among his Jewish Christian brothers. For one, these men were misinformed. Paul never taught Jewish Christians to abandon their Jewish practices. Paul taught Gentile Christians that they needn't become Jewish proselytes (recall Acts 15) in order to fall under grace. Big difference. This wasn't a disagreement about doctrine so much as it was a misunderstanding about praxis, or how one lived out their beliefs. By participating with the four men—and paying their expenses—Paul was reaffirming his respect for Jewish observances. He was not indicating that he believed animal sacrifices were still needed for sins to be forgiven. He merely conceded that Jewish Christians were free to fulfill traditional vows to the Lord as a form of worship, just as Gentiles were free from the obligation to do so in order to be saved. Again, a matter of practice, not doctrine.

How often our Christian disputes center around practices rather than doctrine. How rarely we witness such conciliatory behavior among our brothers and sisters in Christ. Again, there are countless expositions criticizing Paul for his behavior in this instance. They insist that his willingness to offer animal sacrifices at the temple at the end of the fulfillment of this vow nullifies the message of salvation by grace alone. Again, I think that approach is focusing on the wrong character in the plot. Paul is not the protagonist; God is.

First of all, the vow being spoken of is presumably a Nazirite vow. This vow and these sacrifices were not made for the propitiation of sins per se; rather, it was a public display of intentional consecration to the Lord, much like we view baptism. We aren't saved because we are baptized. We're baptized because we have been saved. Second, Paul does not seem to have any issue with taking such vows personally, because he took his own Nazirite vow back at Cenchreae (see Acts 18:18).

Again, we must focus our energy on what this passage is telling us about God, rather than devoting our time and energy judging Paul's heart and actions. First, God expects us to care for the physical needs of our brothers and sisters as readily as those of a spiritual nature. Paul's reason for returning to Jerusalem in large part was to deliver the monetary gift that had been collected from the Gentile churches.

Second, God's heart beats for the solidarity and unity of His church under the lordship of Christ. The Jewish and Gentile churches were vastly dissimilar in their traditions, lifestyle, and thinking and therefore undoubtedly in their practices. Under the direction of the Holy Spirit, Paul tirelessly sought to unify them under the grace of Jesus Christ. He, more than anyone as a devout Jew, understood the cultural and religious roadblocks he was up against in hoping such a thing. Yet because he also understood the enormity and power of his God, he audaciously hoped and relentlessly preached and taught to such an end. In Paul's theology the love of Christ could do immeasurably more than we could imagine!

What are some examples of how we might be called to defer to one another in practices within our churches?

What are some typical areas of practice in which you commonly see division?

When there are disagreements regarding areas of practice within the church, what might be a biblical course of action in order to maintain unity?

In reality, Gentiles were not ever going to be able to offer animal sacrifices inside the temple. Most likely, Jewish Christians were not going to give up all their feasts and other sacred traditions they had practiced for centuries. And neither of them forfeited the grace of Jesus Christ because of it. Nor should either of them boast. Both of them could have pure hearts before God, practicing their forms of worship with hearts of gratitude for what **God had done**. What we read at the beginning of this chapter is also what we must cling to in the end. God is the one who does the work—we are just the repentant sinners, saved by grace. If we became people of *deference* rather than people of *preference,* we'd be a pretty unexplainable church, wouldn't we?

For more insight into Jerusalem, see Deeper Discoveries at ericawiggenhorn.com.

WEEK 8 | DAY 4

BOUND FOR AN AUDIENCE

ACTS 21:27–41

Despite Paul's efforts to build solidarity, opposition arose from non-Christian Jews. Paul had been warned it was coming, and today is when we see Agabus's prophecy come to fulfillment.

Who saw Paul in the temple and where were they from?

What three things did they accuse Paul of teaching against? What assumption did they believe Paul had taken that warranted death?

Who had they seen in the marketplace that led them to this conclusion?

Most likely these Jews were from Ephesus, so they readily recognized Paul along with Trophimus. Although they didn't actually see Trophimus in the temple, they *assumed* Paul had brought him into the temple area with him. How much ruckus has been caused over the centuries due to assumptions rather than facts? And even when we do know the facts concerning what a person may have said and/or done, we still readily apply assumptions as to the why behind the what, namely the motives behind the action.

Within the temple area there was the court of the Gentiles, the court of women, and the area for Jewish men. Signs were posted stating that any non-Jewish male who ventured into either the court of women or the area for Jewish men could be put to death. It was the one situation in which the Jews held the power to execute someone without Roman approval, even a Roman citizen. This accusation against Paul wasn't equivalent to him cutting in line or stepping on someone's toes—he could be killed for this. It was serious business. No wonder the crowds raced to respond!

How did the crowd respond?

What happened to the temple gates?

What was the crowd's intent?

Who came to Paul's rescue?

What actions did the commander take?

Why did Paul have to be taken into the barracks?

Why did the soldiers have to carry Paul?

Write out what the crowd was shouting:

This crowd wanted blood. They had every intention of beating Paul to death. Shutting the gates ensured that Paul's dead body would be separated enough from the temple so as not to desecrate it or make it unclean. During feasts, a Roman garrison would be stationed at the Antonia Fortress, positioned at the northwest corner of temple mount. With a balcony over one hundred feet high, the Romans could adequately view the entire temple area and quickly respond to any unrest. Historically, revolts and civil uprisings occurred during Jewish pilgrimage feasts such as Passover and Pentecost, so presumably the Romans were already on high alert. Regardless, based upon the description of the violence of this crowd, it is quite something that they arrived in time for Paul's life to be spared.

Interestingly, the same chant they made regarding Paul had been previously made in this same exact location about thirty years prior.

Read Luke 23:13–18 and list the similarities between the two scenes.

Before Paul entered the fortress, what question did he ask the commander in Acts 21:37?

How did the commander respond?

What favor did Paul wish the commander to grant him?

Apparently, several years before this an Egyptian Jew claimed to have special powers and told his followers that he would stand on the Mount of Olives and free Jerusalem from Roman rule. In this revolt many of his four thousand followers were killed, but the Egyptian ringleader fled into the desert. The commander assumes Paul is this man and has returned to cause more trouble. When Paul speaks fluent Greek without an Egyptian accent, the commander is surprised. Notice that Paul doesn't tell the commander he is a Roman citizen, only that he is a citizen of Tarsus.

The city of Tarsus was a free Roman city and a center for educational excellence. Citizens of Tarsus held prestige within the Roman world. It wasn't as big of a deal as being a Roman citizen, but it definitely put Paul in a separate class of persons than a lunatic rabble-rouser from Egypt. Since the commander still has no idea why the Jews within the temple are trying to kill Paul, he undoubtedly is wondering exactly what it is that Paul is going to say.

Once Paul receives the commander's permission to speak, what does Paul do and in what language does he address them?

I have tried and tried to picture this scene in my mind and make sense of it. I'm not sure if the crowd had already grown quieter trying to listen to the dialogue between the commander and Paul or some sort of unexplainable hush fell over them. Moments ago this frenzied mob was beating Paul to death. How did they suddenly become silent once Paul motioned to them? After succumbing to such a beating, how did Paul have the physical strength to address them loudly enough to be heard, all while carrying the weight of Roman chains? Something unexplainable is going on here!

Undoubtedly this was a moment for which Paul had yearned for years: the chance to preach the gospel to his Jewish brothers within the walls of their beloved city of Jerusalem. Surely Paul's heart was ready to beat out of his chest hoping with every ounce of his being that they would accept his testimony and the grace offered them through the shed blood of the Lord Jesus. Paul loved these men so deeply. No doubt there were those present in the crowd whom he knew personally. Pharisees who had sat at the feet of Gamaliel alongside him. Elders to whom he had appealed for letters to go and arrest followers of the Way. Those whom he had himself stirred up in anger, dragging Stephen out of the city to stone him. And now he stood as objects of their wrath. He would give anything to be able to convince them of the truth of grace!

Taking a deep breath and choosing his words oh so carefully, he began his testimony . . .

A POWERFUL TESTIMONY

ACTS 22:1–21

Unfortunately for the Roman commander, Paul's use of Aramaic in his testimony probably kept him in the dark. He most likely would not have understood a word Paul was saying. However, hearing Paul speaking to them in their native tongue, a hush fell over the crowd as they realized he was a fellow Jew, familiar with their customs. At this time in Jewish history, many Diaspora Jews, or those who had been scattered, spoke only Greek and very little Hebrew. Palestinian Jews spoke Aramaic, a derivative of Hebrew. Paul's ability to speak to them in this way assured them that he was not merely a Jew by race, but also by practice.

Remember, Paul had been accused of speaking against the Jewish people, the Law of Moses, and the temple.

How does Paul's description of himself in Acts 22:1–5 refute these accusations?

Who else began his defense in this same way in Acts 7:2?

Of what had Stephen been accused according to Acts 6:13?

Some things never change, do they? However, this go around, Paul is standing on the other side of things. He is the defender rather than the accuser.

Read aloud Acts 22:6–11.

Who appeared to Paul and what question did He ask him?

What question did Paul ask in return?

Once he entered Damascus, what would Paul be told?

Somehow I think after witnessing Stephen's death, Paul instinctively knew Jesus was indeed somebody beyond a mere teacher. Paul calls him "Lord," meaning mighty one. I'm not sure Paul was ready to claim Him as the Messiah yet, but he knew there was more to know about Jesus than he currently understood.

Read aloud Acts 22:11–16.

How does Paul describe Ananias?

Why would that description be important to Paul's current audience?

Write out what Ananias told Paul after he restored his sight:

What did Ananias tell Paul to do?

Such a great question! What are you waiting for? How many people have you met over the years who have understood there is more to Jesus than meets the eye? They may not have Him 100 percent figured out yet, but they know He's more than just a teacher or a prophet. He is powerful. He is miraculous. He is worth paying attention to. And yet they just sit there with that discovery. What are they waiting for? It's a head scratcher to me. No doubt Paul was overwhelmed by his discovery. Being a scholar, he probably wished he had all of his rolls of scrolls with him so he could study and research all of the questions running through his mind.

And Ananias simply says, "Paul, stop overthinking it. What you instinctively know, you need to act on!"

How have you seen people overthink Jesus and the simplicity of the gospel?

What do you think prevents people who instinctively know the truth about Jesus from rising up and acting on that knowledge?

Has Jesus ever given you a directive in your life but you failed to act on it because you got stuck overthinking it?

Is there something in your life now in which He is nudging you toward taking action?

Paul did not understand all that was happening to him yet, but he was still called to move forward in faith. Jesus still hadn't finished instructing him.

Read aloud Acts 22:17–22.

Where was Paul the next time Jesus appeared to him and what was Paul doing?

What did Jesus tell him to do?

For what reasons did Paul seem to think his Jewish brethren would believe his testimony?

How did Jesus respond to this argument?

How did the crowd respond to this directive of Jesus to Paul?

This part of the story was the deal breaker for Paul's Jewish audience. Indeed, Jesus had been right. Despite Paul's testimony of how he had relentlessly persecuted followers of Jesus and had now turned to follow Jesus himself, his Jewish brethren rejected his testimony. He was seen as an apostate, one who had rejected his Jewish heritage. It was inconceivable to them that Gentiles could be accepted by God without becoming Jewish proselytes first. It meant their favor as God's special people was no longer true. Gentiles were equal before God under grace? They simply could not accept this.

What do you view as the most common deal breaker for people when it comes to the gospel message?

What part of the message is the hardest for you to accept/grasp/believe personally? Why?

Despite this reaction, Paul would still not give up. He would continue to wrestle before God in prayer for the salvation of his people. And so must we continue to wrestle. Though there are undoubtedly those whom we dearly love who are blind to the truth, the bright light of grace is still able to shine upon them and remove the scales from their eyes. We cannot lose heart. God isn't finished yet.

unexplainable
SIMPLICITY

PIQUED CURIOSITY

ACTS 22:22-30

The moment the door closed behind her mother, it was like somebody flipped a switch. This kindergartner immediately went crazy. She ran around the room throwing things off shelves and ripping things out of her classmates' hands. What triggered the sudden change? Her mother's departure had instantly set her off, and there was no calming her down. A colleague of mine had to come into my classroom to help me contain her as one by one, like a string of dominoes, the rest of my students began to cry and run behind me in fear of being approached by this little girl. Her behavior seemed completely irrational.

Paul's words in verse 22 took the crowd from quiet to chaos in an instant. At the surface of things, we cannot wrap our minds around the sudden change. What was so earthshattering about sending Paul to the Gentiles? Just as with my little kindergartner, we need more information to uncover these intense reactions.

Paul is implying that the Gentiles could be saved without converting to Judaism first. In their minds it is a form of blasphemy, stating that God would offer His promises He had made to Israel to other peoples as well. Throwing dust on your head was a sign of mourning or a response to hearing blasphemy. Taking off one's cloaks could have meant they intended to stone Paul, or it could have been expressing their outrage. At this point, the commander tells his soldiers to drag Paul the rest of the way up the stairs and secure him within the fortress.

The Romans highly valued order. Creating any sort of political disturbance or unrest could get those in charge in serious trouble or even put to death. Because the Jewish people are taking off their cloaks, the commander recognizes that they are communicating that Paul deserves death. The Sanhedrin also removed their cloaks at Stephen's stoning. (For people who were not citizens, Roman soldiers would often flog or whip suspects in order to get them to confess or divulge information.) This also served as a warning against creating any further distur-bances or social havoc.

It wasn't until after he had been fastened in chains for the flogging to commence that Paul raised a very important question.

Write out Acts 22:25 below:

What question did the centurion ask his commander?

There is more implied in this question than meets the eye. The commander has performed a big no-no! Roman citizens were never to be chained until proven guilty. Paul shrewdly concealed his Roman citizenship until after the command-er had chained him. Now Paul has increased his bargaining power with the commander. If Paul were someone important, with friends in high places, this commander could get into serious trouble for putting him in chains. Notice Paul never forfeited his rights under the Roman government; rather he exercised them discriminately and shrewdly.

What did the commander admit to Paul?

How had Paul become a Roman citizen?

During this time there were several ways a person could obtain Roman citizenship.[14] They could be a slave who was freed by their Roman owner and thereby granted Roman citizenship. They could be from a Roman colony, at which point all residents of the colony would be granted citizenship by Rome. (Philippi was one such colony. A colony was a city either founded by the Romans or given privileges as though it had been.[15]) They could have purchased their citizenship due to paying a bribe, as was the case with this commander. Or they could be born a Roman citizen. In other words, they were the son of a Roman citizen, as was the case with Paul. Not all citizenships were considered equal in status. To be born a citizen generally meant you were part of the Roman aristocracy, or somebody who knew important people. This explains why the commander is intent on knowing how Paul obtained his citizenship. He is trying to size him up.

If Paul were an aristocrat, it is quite possible he would know the governor. If the governor found out the commander had put him in chains, the commander himself could be flogged or imprisoned. Paul knew exactly what he was doing in divulging this important piece of information.

How did the soldiers and the commander respond when they discovered Paul's citizenship and how he had obtained it?

The commander is determined to get to the bottom of who Paul is exactly and what all the ruckus is about. However, in the moment of the discovery of Paul's citizenship, he has everyone take a step back and calm down. He needs to come up with a game plan to save his own neck first. It started with removing the chains.

What did the commander do the next day?

This Roman commander has been entrusted with the responsibility to keep the peace in Jerusalem during the feast of Pentecost. During a historically highly volatile time within the walls of Jerusalem, he undoubtedly has political ambitions in demonstrating he can maintain order. This Paul fellow has the crowds screaming for blood and he has to figure out why. If he doesn't somehow punish him, the crowds will not be appeased. He also needs to treat Paul a bit gingerly as a Roman citizen, as well as figure out who his friends in high places are. If Paul claims to have received unfair treatment and he has political connections, it could be curtains for the commander. This commander is going to have to play his cards right to come out on top of this conundrum.

In what way ought we to shrewdly exercise our own rights as American citizens?

In what way ought we also to accept the will of God as Paul did in Acts 21:13?

Paul wrote the book of Romans during his three-month stay in Corinth on his way back to Jerusalem. At this time, he speaks of his plan to go to Rome after he delivers this offering to the church in Jerusalem.

Read Romans 15:23–33.
What did Paul ask the Roman church to do for him?

On a scale of 1 to 10, how certain did he seem of his coming to Rome?

After he stopped in Rome, where did he want to go next?

Paul seems certain the Lord will deliver him and allow him to preach the gospel all the way to Spain. Yet, at the same time, he rests in God's sovereignty over his life and His ability to sweep in and alter events if, when, and how He may see fit. What freedom in this level of surrender!

What hopes and dreams do you wish to see come to fruition in your earthly life?

How would you feel if God swept in and changed the course of your plans?

The paradox of the gospel is that true surrender brings freedom. Submission of our plans opens the door of endless opportunity. It ushers in the unexplainable! If there is something you need to release today, lay it at your Father's feet.

WEEK 9 | DAY 2
SHREWD PERCEPTION
ACTS 23:1–11

The Sanhedrin was the Jewish ruling council that dealt with religious matters. Paul wastes no time beginning his defense before this body and neither shall we in examining his arguments and tactics. There is just too much to discover.

What did Paul claim before the Sanhedrin?

How did the high priest react to Paul's statement?

How did Paul respond in return?

No ceremonial pomp and circumstance nor polite proceedings here. The tension is so thick you can slice it and Paul makes no conciliatory efforts to try to ease it. His statement goes beyond pleading, "Not guilty." He in essence affirms that he has done nothing to defile himself as a Jew and implies that he should not be the one in the assembly bearing the weight of a guilty conscience. Rather, his false accusers should bear the weight of their guilt.

Ananias, the current high priest, was known to be greedy and power hungry. According to Levitical Law a man was not to be struck in the assembly unless he was found guilty. By ordering Paul to be struck before hearing his defense, Ananias broke the law. Paul references Ezekiel 13 in asserting Ananias's guilt.

Read Ezekiel 13:8–16.

What would happen to those whitewashed walls?

What did Jesus say about whitewashed tombs in Matthew 23:27–28?

How did the Sanhedrin respond to Paul's outburst?

Why did Paul apologize?

It is at this point in the discussion Paul immediately changes tactics. Why does he do so? First of all, it is interesting that Paul was unaware that it was the high priest who ordered him to be struck. Several reasons provide possible answers. Since this meeting was convened rather quickly due to the order of the commander, Ananias may have not been adorned in his priestly garments. Since the tension is obviously extremely high, it is difficult to know how orderly this proceeding took place. There could have been so much whispering or shouting that Paul did not see who exactly ordered him to be struck.

Tradition also tells us that Paul suffered from poor eyesight, though this is just speculation, in which case he may have been unable to distinguish who signaled the order. Another possibility is that Paul *did* know who Ananias was, and that he had a reputation for being one of most corrupt and evil high priests to hold the office, so his response to him was an intentional insult. Yet another interpretation of events is that Paul really did not know who Ananias was, and that when he realized his error, he acknowledged it. What we can infer is that since no one in the Sanhedrin seemed to speak out against the violation of the law that occurred in striking Paul, he quickly assessed the entire crowd to be hostile toward him. Remember, these men were trying to kill Paul yesterday because they claimed to be zealous for the law. Yet here they stood openly breaking the law without batting an eye. Paul could see the writing on the wall and that no matter how logical of a defense he presented, they had already declared him guilty.

At this point, what did Paul claim this trial was really about?

What happened after he made this claim?

Upon which two issues do the Sadducees and Pharisees predominantly disagree?

To what conclusion did the Pharisees arrive?

What did the commander do as a result?

What did Jesus promise Paul that night in a vision?

For two days in a row now Paul has nearly been beaten to death and ripped to shreds. The Jews were so riled up he realized he couldn't even attempt to reason with them. This must have broken his heart. I am sure he hoped that upon his return to Jerusalem he would have the opportunity to clearly present the message of Christ, but as soon as he had mentioned Gentile inclusion it was all over. The opportunity had passed. Their ears and minds were closed.

Paul also probably realized the commander was not going to release him any time soon. With the Jews in such a frenzy it would cause way too much of an uproar to simply dismiss this case. He would have to either figure out a way to indict Paul so he could punish him to appease the Jewish mobs or offer them something else they wanted in return to make them calm down. Since the commander could not think of anything for which he could find Paul guilty, he was in a tough spot politically.

Read Luke 23:13–23.

Note the similarities in Jesus' and Paul's situations:

I'm quite certain the similarities were not lost on Paul either. No wonder Jesus came and appeared to Paul. The entire scene was history repeating itself all over again. Unlike Jesus, however, Paul's Roman citizenship guarded against him being punished unjustly. However, he also knew that Jesus had been crucified unjustly and Jewish mobs had persuaded Roman law in the past. Though he appeared to be in a no-win situation, Jesus assured him that he would still have the opportunity to go to Rome.

Have you ever found yourself in a no-win situation? What would it look like for you to take courage?

Tomorrow we will see the incredible twist of circumstances that releases Paul from the Jews in Jerusalem. It certainly was not by any means Paul could have predicted. The zeal of this mob escalated to such a height they ended up foiling their own plans. And is that not the way of our God? He takes the snares of our enemy and entangles him within his very own nets.

What warning did God issue in Isaiah 29:20–21?

What advice is given in Proverbs 6:2–4?

Our God can do the impossible. What seems like a no-win, no-way-out situation to our human understanding is precisely the circumstance where God steps in to do the unexplainable!

> Deeper Discoveries at ericawiggenhorn.com tell more about the Pharisees and Sadducees.

WEEK 9 | DAY 3
FOILED PLANS
ACTS 23:12–24:27

I would say the greatest resolve anyone could take toward a cause or belief would be a willingness to die for it, wouldn't you? The Jews concoct a plan to ensure Paul's assassination, and in the event it was executed, it certainly would have meant death for at least some of the Jews involved in the plot. To ambush Roman guards transporting Paul meant a willingness to put their own lives in danger. This gives us a vivid picture as to how vehemently they disagreed with Paul and his message of grace in Christ Jesus.

What plot did the Jews concoct and which groups of people were involved?

How did they express their resolve to ensure Paul's death?

Who discovered this plot and what action did he take?

How did Paul respond to news of this plot?

How did the commander respond?

What reasons did Lysias cite in his letter for sending Paul to Governor Felix?

There are so many unanswered questions in this narrative. First of all, who is Paul's nephew and how in the world did he obtain the inside scoop regarding this plot? He may have been a student of a Pharisee, since Paul's father was a Pharisee as well as Paul. Or he may have merely happened to be at the right place at the right time. Regardless, we see miraculous intervention at several levels. First, that this young man discovered the plot. Second, that Paul had found enough favor in the centurion's eyes that he took his nephew to the commander to report this. Third, that the commander dispatched nearly five hundred Roman soldiers to guarantee Paul's safe arrival to Caesarea, which was over sixty miles away.

Remember, this was occurring during the time of Pentecost. Tensions were high in Jerusalem, and the commander's only goal was to keep peace in the city. Dispatching such a large number of soldiers certainly diminished the military muscle at the Antonia Fortress. However, squelching this Paul hubbub probably was at the top of his list in peace-keeping goals. By removing Paul from Jerusalem, he had removed the potential for more rioting.

What decision did Governor Felix make in regard to hearing Paul's case?

Of what three things did Tertullus accuse Paul?

What point do you suppose Paul was trying to make in saying that it was no more than twelve days ago since he arrived in Jerusalem?

To what things did Paul admit in response to Tertullus's accusations?

For what reason had Paul come to Jerusalem?

Whose attendance did Paul assert was necessary for this trial to be fair?

For what reason did Paul claim he was actually on trial?

The genius of Paul's rhetoric shines brightly in this passage. Tertullus claims that Paul's character as a troublemaker preceded his arrival to Jerusalem. His motives for coming to their holy city were to desecrate the temple, and the religion that Paul teaches should be disassociated from Judaism. He wanted it considered an illegal religion under Roman law, namely it should be deemed a secret society—organizations that Rome explicitly prohibited under their law.

Instead of directly refuting these arguments, Paul does something probably no one expected—he confesses that he is indeed a member of a so-called sect. But his intent is to prove once again that Christianity, or followers of the Way, are a part of Judaism and should be regarded as protected under Roman law.

Paul begins by stating that his arrival to Jerusalem served a two-fold purpose: he came to worship and to bring alms for the poor. Both of these actions proved his devout character. Second, under Roman law, accusers were required to present eyewitnesses to bear proof of their accusations. Therefore, Paul says, "If you are going to accuse me of desecrating the temple, then the two men from the province of Asia who started this whole mess should be present!" Since they were not, the accusations were not justifiable. Also under Roman law, any accusations needed to be consistent in the development of a case. Paul in essence is saying, "The Sanhedrin put me on trial for preaching the resurrection of the dead; now today you are putting me on trial for desecrating the temple. Which accusation is it? You cannot continue to change the reasons for my case." Because Felix was familiar with the teachings of the Way, Paul attempts to convince him that this is merely a religious dispute over the doctrine of resurrection, not a new, illicit religion unsanctioned by Roman law.

What decision did Governor Felix make regarding Paul's case?

How did Felix respond to Paul's preaching? How do you account for his reaction?

What was Felix secretly hoping?

For how long did Paul stay a prisoner in Herod's palace at Caesarea?

Felix's corruption is illustrated in these last two verses. Under Roman law any case not concluded after two years should be dropped.[16] However, Felix continued to keep Paul imprisoned. His verdict in waiting for Lysias's arrival served nothing more than an expert stalling mechanism. He knew full well that until he summoned Lysias himself, the trial would remain stagnant. From extrabiblical sources we know that members of the Judean aristocracy reported Governor Felix to Rome, accusing him of improper governance. He was known as ruthless and crooked in his dealings. No doubt he failed to release Paul knowing full well that to do so would cause backlash from the Jews. Felix could not afford any more hand slapping from Roman officials.

Eventually Felix lost his governorship over Judea and was replaced by Festus. During these two years Paul remained imprisoned within the walls of Herod's palace at Caesarea, yet the work of the church continued. Think of the development of the several church leaders we have already encountered through these pages of Scripture: Timothy, John Mark, Trophimus, Apollos, Gaius, and many others, both named and unnamed. These men needed to step in and take greater leadership roles now that Paul was imprisoned. Knowing Paul would hear of their progress, they had accountability while still developing their leadership skills. Just think of the location of Paul's imprisonment—not too far away from Jerusalem and easily reached by boat for all of the churches in Greece, Pamphylia, and Asia Minor. Was this a mere coincidence? I don't think so. Paul was centrally located those two years in a place where any and every one of his churches could reach him. Apparently he was allowed visitors (24:23).

Paul's imprisonment afforded them time to step up to the plate without having to grieve Paul's final absence. They could still communicate with him. He wasn't gone forever. Paul was still accessible. Not easily accessible, mind you, but accessible nonetheless. As issues arose, Paul could be consulted. Could it be that part of Paul's imprisonment also afforded these men to whom he would soon pass the baton of leadership a greater time of preparation?

While on the surface of things Paul's imprisonment may have appeared to be an endless waiting game, if we widen the lens slightly we can infer God used it for a mighty purpose within His kingdom.

Are you waiting for something today, friend? Are you willing to concede that God may indeed be using the wait for purposes beyond what is currently in your immediate view? Often the purpose behind the wait is the most unexplainable part of all!

Before you close today, journal your thoughts below:

A PURPOSEFUL APPEAL

ACTS 25:1–27

Paul is detained indefinitely in Caesarea in Herod's palace under Felix's jurisdiction. This wicked governor is replaced, however, after complaints to Rome for his poor governance. The Senate ousts Felix and he is replaced by Festus. One of the first things Festus does on arrival to his new appointment as governor of Syrian Judea is visit Jerusalem. A political move, no doubt, since it was the Jewish aristocracy who had sought Felix's removal. Seizing their opportunity, Paul's enemies immediately get to work.

What request did the Jews in Jerusalem make of Festus regarding Paul?

How did Festus answer them?

How quickly did Festus make good on his word to bring Paul to trial?

List the three things Paul defends himself against in verse 8:

Why do you suppose it would have been favorable to the Jews to have Festus try Paul within Jerusalem?

Based on the question Festus asked regarding the location of the trial and Paul's defense summary in verse 8, we can infer a couple of things. First of all, we already know the chief priests and Jews initially accused Paul of desecrating the temple by suggesting he brought Trophimus the Ephesian inside the inner court where only Jewish males were allowed entrance. Second, Tertullus sought to make the claim that Paul was teaching an illegal religion—a religion separate from Judaism, thus breaking Roman law. It seems, however, that during this go-around they also brought additional accusations that had not been previously mentioned under the trial with Lysias or Felix. These charges involved breaking a law specifically against Caesar.

As a Roman governor, Festus presumably struggled to follow much of the conversation. He was not versed in Jewish law or theology. While wanting to establish good relations with the Jewish aristocracy and get his reign off on the right foot, he also didn't want to jeopardize his legitimacy as a just upholder of Roman laws. At this point the Jews accused Paul of many things but were unable to actually prove any of them.

How did Paul respond to the suggestion from Festus that he be tried in Jerusalem?

As a Roman citizen Paul held the right to bring his case before the emperor. This appeal isn't the same as what we think of in our justice system today where you disagree with your sentencing and thus appeal to a higher court. This right held by Roman citizens implied their fear that justice would be denied them in the court of law in which they were being tried. The citizen did not deem the current ruler able to arrive at an unbiased judgment. I think Paul clearly realized Festus might cater to the Jews, at which point he would most likely face an ambush and death without a trial.

How did Festus respond to Paul's appeal to Caesar?

On the one hand this gives Festus the green light to get rid of the Paul problem. Festus could simply say to the Jews, "He has appealed to Caesar, so there's nothing more I can do." On the other hand, Festus looks slightly incompetent. He hasn't maintained jurisdiction over this area for even a month and he already has a prisoner demanding the audience of his imperial majesty—one who has undergone three trials already and has yet to be found guilty in any of them. How is Festus going to send him to trial in Rome when none of the accusations against him are even going to hold up in court? Indeed, this is a problem for Festus, but he has a plan.

Who comes to visit Festus?

How did Festus explain his problem to Agrippa?

What do you think Festus means when he says "until I could send him to Caesar" in verse 21?

How did Agrippa respond to Festus' story about Paul?

What is Festus' goal in bringing Paul before Agrippa, according to verse 26?

In other words, Festus has no idea exactly what the charges are to include in his correspondence to the emperor. Something about a dead man named Jesus who Paul claimed was alive. He had no idea what they were talking about and certainly didn't see why it led the Jews to want to kill Paul. Agrippa, however, was a Jew himself. Maybe he could explain this to Festus. He was also educated, so he understood Roman law as well. He was the perfect person to unravel this mess and help Festus come up with reasonable charges that would cast him in a good light in the eyes of the emperor.

How well do you think Paul understood the purpose of this trial? Why do you believe as you do?

Tomorrow we are going to read through Paul's defense. We will see that his message was directed toward Agrippa much more than at Festus. Frankly, I don't think Paul concerned himself with what charges these two men would establish against him. He welcomed this opportunity to witness to the ruler of the Jewish nobility—the very man who held the power to select the Jewish high priest for the temple of Jerusalem. Paul knew he was going to Rome one way or the other. This trial, however, was presumably his very last opportunity to preach to his Jewish brothers, hoping to convince them that Jesus was the Messiah for whom they had all been waiting.

ONE LAST SERMON

ACTS 26:1–32

With great pomp and revelry Agrippa and his sister Bernice were ushered into the amphitheater, followed by Governor Festus and the commanding tribunes of Caesarea. Seated in their regalia in their assigned seats for the nobles, countless others found a seat within the amphitheater as well, their curiosity piqued. Jewish aristocracy from Jerusalem sat below, seething for the chance for Paul to be sentenced to death. Who knows how many came to watch the scene? Certainly Agrippa and Bernice wouldn't have taken measures to enter with such pomp for an audience of one: Paul.

Then Paul is brought in. One arm chained to a Roman guard, dressed in a simple prisoner's tunic, he slowly takes the three steps up to the stage so he can be effectively heard. As the audience lays eyes upon him they are shocked. He appears so insignificant in stature and unremarkable in appearance (see 2 Corinthians 10:10). How could this be Paul, the rebel Pharisee? The one who had created such a stir among the Jews and was so dearly loved by those of the Way? Perhaps Philip was sitting in this crowd as well as his daughters, along with the rest of the believers of the city, praying for Paul to have wisdom and protection. Certainly the outcome of this case could greatly affect their freedom to continue to worship Jesus. Christianity currently held protection under the Roman law, but would that change after today?

As Paul turned to face Agrippa, a hush fell over the crowd. Paul took a deep breath, stretched his hand in a gesture of respect for the king, and addressed Agrippa personally rather than the crowd at large.

For what reasons did Paul consider himself fortunate to have Agrippa serve as judge in this trial?

What did Paul claim his accusers knew in regard to his character?

For what reason did Paul say he was on trial?

How did Paul assert that resurrection was an ancient Jewish idea?

How does Paul's explanation that he was a devout Jew and avid student of the Scriptures, yet had still misunderstood Jesus' claims, give his current audience an "out" so to speak for not believing in Jesus?

Under Jewish law, atonement could be provided for those who committed unintentional sins. There was no atonement for those who willfully sinned (see note 1). In Paul's opening, he offers his listeners, including Agrippa, much grace. He essentially admits that it is possible to be a good, devout, blameless Jew and miss Jesus as the Messiah. In other words, their failure to recognize Him could be viewed as atonable under the law as an unintentional sin.

From here, Paul moves into how he discovered Jesus as Messiah. This is the third time Paul shares his testimony. Each time it varies slightly depending upon the audience with whom Paul shares it, but the overarching story remains the same.

Let's look at some of the unique aspects of his testimony before Herod.

What does Jesus tell Paul to stop kicking against? See verse 14.

This comes from a Greek proverb in regard to the futility of fighting against a deity.[17] Since Herod Agrippa received a classical Greek education, he would understand the allusion Paul presented here. Paul implies Christ's deity here and that Jesus' mission is of God since he links the persecution of Jesus to an attack against God.

Write out Acts 26:16 here:

Several elements of this verse imply a prophetic or apostolic call according to Jewish thought.

Read Ezekiel 2:1–5 and Acts 26:16–17.
Note the similarities between the two callings in the chart below.

EZEKIEL'S CALL	PAUL'S CALL

At this point, Paul switches to decidedly Messianic language and begins to quote the prophet Isaiah. He compares the work that Jesus commanded of him to the prophecies concerning the work of the Messiah.

Match the following verses with the work Paul was called by Jesus to perform.

OPEN THE EYES OF THE BLIND	ISAIAH 35:5–6
TURN THEM FROM DARKNESS TO LIGHT	ISAIAH 42:6–7, 16
RECEIVE A PLACE AMONG THE SANCTIFIED	ISAIAH 61:1–2
RECEIVE FORGIVENESS OF SINS	ISAIAH 61:10–11
RELEASE THEM FROM THE POWER OF SATAN (ENEMIES) TO GOD	ISAIAH 56

Paul has been called by a heavenly vision to continue the work of Jesus on earth. And what is the work of Jesus? The promises that were to be ushered in with the coming of Messiah. In Jewish thought, once the Messiah came, He would again establish the nation of Israel as an independent nation. Because Agrippa is quite familiar with Jewish prophecies concerning the Messiah, Paul deliberately refers to them in his defense.

According to Paul, what should one do once he has repented?

How does Paul again insist that he is not preaching another god other than Yahweh, nor a new doctrine other than the ancient Messianic promises?

What did Paul say the Christ would do in Acts 26:23?

Who interrupted Paul at this point and what did he suggest?

For what reason did Paul claim he could speak openly regarding his beliefs?

What question did he ask Agrippa?

How did Agrippa respond?

This is the longest of all of Paul's sermons . . . or shall we say speeches of defense? He is pulling out all the stops. This is his last shot to explain Jesus as Messiah to his Jewish brethren and he is going to give it all he's got. He is brazen enough to ask Agrippa a direct question: "You believe in the ancient prophecies, don't you, Agrippa?" To our Western ears this seems benign enough. We might translate it, "Are you tracking with me, here?" but in the current context, Paul essentially says his teachings did not occur secretively in a little corner and then he turns around and immediately backs Agrippa into one. A gasp must have let out across the crowd, along with a hush as to how Agrippa would respond.

If Agrippa were to say, "No," then he is essentially denouncing his Judaism, which would have caused an uproar with the Jews present at the trial. If he says, "Why, yes, of course I do. I am as good a Jew as the next man!" then he has essentially declared himself to be as mad as Paul and he tosses out all respect from the Romans. There is not a good answer to this question. He is backed up against the wall and Paul no doubt knows he expertly put him there by posing the question to him in the first place.

These are the times I wish I had an audio Bible. Because it is in these moments that tone would mean everything. Is Agrippa sarcastic in his response? Does he chuckle at the cleverness of Paul? Does he burst out in anger at being outsmarted by Paul in his rhetoric? We don't know for sure, but Agrippa demonstrates his own rhetorical prowess by answering Paul's question with a question of his own.

What question does Agrippa ask Paul?

Paul straightens up and locks his eyes upon Agrippa, seated high above him in the noble's box. *Ah yes, if you only knew, Agrippa, how desperately I wish I could turn your heart to make you a follower of Jesus! It is my aim in life that I might present Jesus so clearly, with such expertly framed arguments, by a spotless life, and through my endless tears and petitions to the throne of grace, that indeed you, Agrippa, along with all of my Jewish brothers might become Christians.* This is the heart of Paul. Indeed, he would explain the Scriptures to Agrippa for as long as he needed if it meant he came to repentance. Paul would trade nothing on earth for his salvation. So Paul smiles and says, "I pray everyone here becomes like me," then raises his right arm as the heavy chain clinks and echoes in the silent amphitheater, "except without these chains, of course!"

Now sighs of relief are heard as the mood shifts. I imagine Paul expertly brought in humor to ease the tension. Agrippa, however, is done listening. He rises, immediately followed by the governor and his sister Bernice. He has heard enough. He's not about to get backed into another corner. Paul does not deserve death, nor even imprisonment. If he had not appealed to Caesar, he could have been released.

Now this is seriously good news for followers of Jesus. The Judean king has now agreed with Roman law. This is the man who appoints the high priest. If Agrippa is unwilling to back their accusations, their case is lost. Not only that, but there may have been some fear in going against Agrippa's ruling of Paul's innocence. The

Jews' ability to get the Romans to view Christianity as a religion apart from Judaism has been squelched. The Jewish king himself has said otherwise. Yet again we see the unexplainable sovereignty of God protect His church. We may have lots of people out there kicking against the goads trying to stop the gospel, but God will still provide a way for His message to go forth.

unexplainable
COMMUNITY

WEEK 10 | DAY 1
OFF TO ROME
ACTS 27:1–12

One thing I cannot help but notice is how Paul's upbringing aided him countless times in his mission. An expert in the law, he could debate with the Jews. Highly educated, fluent in Greek, he could preach to the Gentiles, engage in respectful rhetoric with Roman aristocracy and, when needed, pull out the trump card of his Roman citizenship. He was at home among both groups of people. A laboring man, he was also home among commoners as well as the educational, political, and religious elite. Truly a jack of all trades, so to speak. No part of his life was wasted; rather, it was divinely orchestrated by God to prepare him for the ministry with which he would be entrusted. Even his own rebellion against the followers of the Way was later used by God as convincing proof of his certainty that Jesus was indeed the promised Messiah. Unexplainable!

Think of your own life experiences—where you grew up, where you went to school or what you studied. What you do for a living.

How could these things be seen as tools to help you fulfill God's kingdom plans He wants to do through you?

How might He redeem your rebellion?

How might He bring triumph out of tragedy?

How might He use your life experiences to impact others?

How could He use your disappointment to help someone else pursue their dreams?

Though it took many, many years for Paul to step into the fullness of His calling from God, not one single step had been wasted. (See Acts 11:25–26, when Barnabas went to Paul's hometown of Tarsus to find him and bring him back to Antioch, to begin to shepherd the predominantly Gentile church there.) God in His great way made use of it all! What an incredible encouragement that is. Last week we concluded with what, as far as we know, was Paul's final sermon—in actuality a defense speech—he was ever to preach in Judea. Through that speech we see God securely protecting the church through Agrippa's conclusion that Paul's message did not deserve either death or imprisonment. This was not good news for the Jews in Jerusalem. All of their "kicking against the goads" (fighting against God's will; recall Acts 26:14) had gotten them nowhere. The gospel was free to spread under the auspices of Roman protection due to its link to Judaism. With this verdict, Paul is ready to go to Rome.

Read aloud Acts 27:1–12.

Who were Paul's traveling companions on this first part of the voyage?

What did Julius allow Paul to do in Sidon?

Roman prisoners weren't given food and clothing like they are in American prisons. If Paul were to eat, somebody was going to have to come feed him or provide funding for the food. And Roman guards generally weren't too sympathetic to their plight. Paul has been imprisoned for over two years now. Roman guards generally didn't let their prisoners "go visit friends" either. Paul, however, has a long journey ahead and is going to need a fair amount of provision in order to arrive in Rome without starving to death. Somehow Julius is able to sense Paul's determination to make it to Rome. He's going to make sure he gets back on the ship before it sets sail. What a beautiful picture of these churches in which Paul has so tirelessly served, now turning around and caring for him. Not only that, but Luke and Aristarchus also came along, no doubt to help Paul carry his beloved parchments and writing tools, so he could continue to shepherd his churches via letters. Aristarchus also had been Paul's traveling companion in Ephesus and had been seized within the amphitheater during the riot over Artemis.

In what ways could the church do a better job of caring for the needs of our pastors?

So the journey continues.

What ship did Paul and his companions board next?

What happened on this ship?

Why did Paul warn the captain and sailors?

Which two men in particular wanted to continue sailing?

What was the final decision?

By the time they reached Fair Haven it was just past Yom Kippur, or the Day of Atonement (referred to in v. 9). This Jewish holiday is celebrated in the fall, so winter is approaching quickly. Ships did not generally sail in the winter, but would dock during these months and then begin traveling again in the spring. The ship's owner and captain, however, wished to arrive in Rome before winter in order to unload their cargo and no doubt to also receive payment for their wares. Paul, who had already been shipwrecked three times (2 Corinthians 11:25), could tell this was going to be a disastrous decision and warned them against it.

I think the mention of the Day of Atonement holds more significance than just giving us a timeline. This Jewish holiday signified the holiest day of the year. The Jewish people felt they were closer to God on this day than any of the other Jewish holidays. Part of the celebration included the reading of the book of Jonah. Who was he again? Oh yeah, the first prophet to the Gentiles . . . the wicked Assyrians. Where was Paul trying to go? To preach to the pagan city of Rome. Just as the Assyrians under Jonah represented the ruthless rulers over Israel, so Rome represented the current subjugation of Israel. Yom Kippur was a day of purification and rededication of oneself to God. No doubt Paul needed to undergo some emotional and spiritual dedication for what lay ahead for him.

In our Christian traditions, communion would probably be the closest celebration we have to the Day of Atonement. We confess our sin, remember God's forgiveness in Christ, and dedicate ourselves to His kingdom in repentance. Most Christians would probably say that when they participate in communion they feel particularly close to God. But what would it be like to set aside an entire day to purify and rededicate ourselves to God? To dwell on God's sacrifice for our forgiveness?

When was the last time, if ever, you took a day and set it aside solely to focus on God?

How do you think it could benefit your spiritual growth to do so?

I have a friend who takes at least one DAWG day every year: a Day Alone With God. She writes out all her activities, commitments, responsibilities, plans, dreams, and goals and lays them out symbolically before the Lord, lifting each one up to Him in prayer. There's nothing magical about laying them out, it just helps her to visualize the call to offer them all up to the Lord to guide and direct as He will. It is Romans 12:1–2 in a literal sense.

Look up Romans 12:1–2 and write it out here:

On a scale from 1 to 10, with how much certainty can you say you are following the will of God with your life?

Paul knew 100 percent he was supposed to go to Rome. This was God's plan for him and while he willingly obeyed, he was also realistic about the difficulty he would face. He wisely prepared, bringing along traveling companions to aid him, and tangible provision to sustain him. He thought through the cost of obedience and prepared himself as best he could. He also trusted God with the unknowns. He purified himself, dedicated himself, and resolutely moved forward in faith to the glorious center of the empire: the great city of Rome!

To read more about Rome, see Deeper Discoveries at ericawiggenhorn.com.

As you think about your own journey with God, ponder the following questions and present them before Him:

Am I diligently and intentionally preparing myself for what You have in store for me, God?

Am I wise in preparing to serve You in whatever capacity to which You may call me?

Am I certain that whatever unknowns I may face, I can trust You to work out those details?

Am I resolutely pursuing a life of obedience toward You, no matter what difficulty I might face?

Those are tough questions, friend. I applaud you for even considering how you might answer them. The truth is that in this life, whether we follow God or not, we are going to face difficulty. We live in a sinful world, with loss, tragedy, and death. But this world is not our home. And we are not left to the whims of the world. We have a Father in heaven who watches over us, provides for us, and cares for us every step of the way. That doesn't mean there won't be difficulty, but it does mean that there will *always* be hope. And if there is anything we have learned about the Unexplainable Church, it's that when we are in the center of God's will, we are unstoppable!

TAKE HEART

ACTS 27:13–38

We left off right in the middle of Paul's voyage and I'm sure you are as anxious for him to get to Rome as I am, so let's jump right back aboard today, shall we?

What happened soon after they left the harbor in Crete?

Based on Acts 27:14–17, how strong do you suppose these winds were? The word used for the wind in verse 14 is *typhonikos*, or *typhonic*.

What did the men throw overboard the following two days?

Read Jonah 1:1–16 and compare it with what is happening on the ship Paul is on.
What did the sailors in both of these stories do because of the storm?

In the story of Jonah, who was blamed for the storm and why?

Read Jonah's prayer in Jonah 2:1–9. In what specific elements of this prayer might Paul have found great comfort?

Describe the state of mind of the sailors in Acts 27:20:

Contrast it with Paul's state of mind:

How was Paul so certain they would be spared?

Write out Acts 27:25 here:

Now complete the following:

So, keep up your courage, _____, for I have
(write your name here)
faith in God that _____

_____

(fill in a circumstance for which you need courage and faith right now)

Now I haven't had any angelic visions, but this much I do know: whatever God has promised us in His Word, we can bank on it!

So what are some of those promises?

— He will complete what He started (Philippians 1:6).

— He will never leave you or forsake you (Deuteronomy 31:6).

— His discipline is for our good (Hebrews 12:10).

—He will one day present us to His Father (Jude 24).

—He is always at work (John 5:17).

Circle the promises above that bring you courage at this time.

Oftentimes courage involves waiting. The promises delivered through Paul's vision did not immediately come to fruition. For another fourteen days these sailors bravely fought the wind and waves hoping to find a place to land. An interesting change occurs here, though. These sailors did something that hasn't been previously mentioned.

Look carefully at Acts 27:29, what did these sailors do?

Well, that sounds good, doesn't it? We like to hear about people praying in a crisis. Unfortunately, as soon as the crisis becomes manageable, people often stop praying and start scheming instead.

What did the sailors decide to do next?

How did Paul react to this scheme?

Now for the life of me, I can't figure out how Paul worked this out. I'm not sure if he had so much sea experience at this point he instinctively knew these sailors were messing with the life boat, or if the Holy Spirit revealed their plot to him supernaturally. Paul's discovery isn't the most amazing part anyway. What's amazing is that these men actually listened to Paul! They believed what he told them, and they believed it enough to bet their life on it.

Write out Acts 27:31:

Of what did Paul assure them when they finally ate?

How did the crew respond to Paul's words?

What did they do when they had finished eating?

How does this further demonstrate they believed Paul's words?

Paul's faith served as such an encouragement to the men on this ship. They didn't know the story of Jonah. They probably didn't know the Scriptures. And until they met Paul, quite likely, they didn't know Jesus. Yet over the course of the last fourteen days, Paul's steadfast faith had served them well. He knew they were going to make it to Rome. They had lost hope, but Paul remained hopeful. Jesus had told him he would make it to Rome.

In what context did Jesus use the term "the hairs on your head" in Matthew 10:28–31?

Paul was certain that if God had been able to spare his life from all of the repeated attacks of the Jews, God could certainly spare him on the sea. Jesus had calmed the sea with a word, so what did Paul have to fear? Not a single one of the men would be lost. They would all arrive safely. But they were expected to work together to ensure they all made it to shore. What a beautiful picture of our promise of heaven! Indeed, no matter what storms we face or who may come against us, our Father will bring us home to safety where there will be no more sickness, death, crying, or pain. And until we arrive, He watches over us so closely, even the very hairs on our head are numbered.

WEEK 10 | DAY 3
NOT ONE LOST
ACTS 27:39–ACTS 28:10

Yesterday the tide had begun to turn—literally. The men knew they were approaching land. Paul assured them they would all survive and not one lose "a single hair from his head." This old Jewish proverb came from the belief that protection would be granted to those who behaved honorably. (See 1 Samuel 14:45; 2 Samuel 14:11; 1 Kings 1:52.) We will discover, however, that certain fellows aboard concocted a dishonorable plan.

What did the soldiers plan on doing with the prisoners once the ship ran aground?

Who interceded to prevent Paul's death?

If you ever watched *Titanic*, you know that clinging to a ship's plank to help you float was no guarantee of survival. We were already told that the waves were so harsh they were battering the ship to pieces after it rammed into the sand bar. They are cast into dangerous, swirling sea water with giant waves. Jumping in to swim to shore wasn't going to be anything like swimming laps at the YMCA. For all 276 of them to reach shore safely was nothing short of miraculous. Let's not forget they have battled this storm for over two weeks and consumed only one meal. Exhausted, tired, probably dehydrated and weakened by hunger, somehow every last one of them arrived safely—just had Paul had told them.

Where did Paul and the others land?

How is the hospitality of these people described?

What happened to Paul as he helped prepare the fire?

To what conclusion did the islanders arrive regarding the person of Paul?

What did Paul do to the snake?

Then what did the islanders conclude?

Shipwrecks were common at this time in history. Archaeologists have found remains from over one thousand ships in this area of the sea. Also common was superstition and divination. Many people believed that when someone survived a shipwreck, it was evidence of their noble character. They could even cite shipwreck survival as a defense of their character or religious purity within a courtroom.[18] It is no wonder Paul cites that he was shipwrecked three times to the Corinthians when they challenge his apostleship. It also explains why the people of Malta expressed such gracious hospitality. For every single crew member to defy death and arrive safely upon their island after such a horrific storm signified that someone aboard must hold great favor with the gods.

After Paul suffered no ill effects from the viper wrapped around his arm, they concluded the righteous fellow must be Paul.

Who offered hospitality?

Since Luke says he received "us," he could have meant Paul and his companions, or he could have meant all 276 men from the ship. In any case, what did Paul do for Publius's father?

What did the rest of the islanders do after this incident?

To show Paul their thanks, what did they do before they left?

In ancient times those who performed "miracles" often received payment for their services. Generally, God's prophets did not accept payment for any miracles performed. Jesus told his disciples not to accept any form of payment for any miracles they performed in His Name (see Matthew 10:8). So why did Paul accept recompense in this instance?

I think Paul accepted food and supplies for the journey, which was considered hospitality more than payment. He also may have had no choice, because the Roman officials may have offered it to Julius, rather than Paul. The beauty to behold is God's care in Paul's daily provision under the safety and care of the islanders at Malta as well as in the raging sea.

Is it easier for you to notice God's care and provision in times of great crisis or in daily, run-of-the-mill life? How so?

How do you see people making judgment of others' character based on their "fortune" or "lot in life" like the islanders did with Paul?

After all of these 276 people survived this shipwreck with Paul, witnessed his miracles, and saw God's hand of protection over them, how many of them do you think came to faith in Christ?

If they did not believe Paul's message of salvation, what do you think prevented them from doing so?

Well now it is time for them to head out to sea once again. And as we'll read tomorrow, there are many things in which people may place their faith, but according to Paul, Jesus is the only one worthy to receive it.

ONE LAST APPEAL

ACTS 28:11–29

I remember it like it was yesterday. My shiny, metallic-blue bicycle stood proudly in the driveway. A white banana seat with pink flowers, matching pink pompoms hanging from the handlebars, and a white basket on the front. My very first big-girl bike. This was the first morning, however, that the kickstand was needed. My dad had taken off my training wheels and it was do-or-die time. I hopped on my bike and began pedaling, slowly at first and then faster as my confidence soared. I went all the way around the block, so proud of myself I could burst. As I neared our home and pulled into the driveway, I was going way too fast. Panic swept over me when I realized I couldn't slow down soon enough. I crashed right into our picket fence, smashing my basket and splintering my hands and face. Skinned knees, a broken heart, and a mangled front tire; my pride was crushed.

I wonder how Paul and company felt boarding this new ship for the next leg of their journey. Were they nervous? Eager to arrive in Rome? Ready for the challenge? Panic stricken? Crushed pride, remembering the rash promises they had made and had yet to follow through on? How many of them had uttered promises to Paul's god that if he saved them, they would repent of their sins? Luke, never one to throw in details without trying to make a point, tells us two things about this ship: it was Alexandrian and it had the twin gods Castor and Pollux on the helm. Why does he mention these things?

Alexandrian ships came from Alexandria, Egypt. Ancients coined Alexandria as the "bread basket of Rome." These large ships came loaded with grain to the capital city. Every citizen in Rome received free grain, as Rome highly prized order and stability. Hungry people generally tend to be less stable and harder to control. These ships would sail directly north toward modern-day Turkey and then west along the coast to arrive in Rome. Generally quite large, this ship was probably bigger in size than the previous ship they had boarded at Adramyttium (27:2).

The twin gods Castor and Pollux were Rome's patron gods of mariners. They were often supplicated for fair winds and favorable weather conditions for smooth sailing. After their miraculous deliverance from the previous storm at the promise and intervention of Yahweh, relying on a ship's size or false gods for safe passage is heralded as ridiculous. No-nonsense Dr. Luke alerts us to the futile things in which man will foolishly put his trust. From the moment of Paul's initial arrest in the temple, the theme of God's sovereign protection and intervention carries on like a never-ending seashore. The ship does, however, make exceptional time and they arrive in Puteoli.

For how long had Paul and crew remained on Malta?

Whom did they meet at Puteoli?

Puteoli was about 130 miles south of Rome. At this port they disembarked and presumably made the rest of their journey on land. Christianity had spread this far outside of Rome already. This provides a beautiful glimpse into the evangelism efforts of these early believers. The church in Rome had presumably taken the gospel over 130 miles from the city center. That may not seem that far by today's standards, but with most travel done on foot, that would be at least a ten-day journey. These early believers received the good news of the gospel with such joy they couldn't help but share it with others—even when it included sacrifice.

From whom did you originally hear the gospel?

On a scale from 1 to 10, how much sacrifice was involved in them bringing the message of the gospel to you?

1	5	10
LITTLE SACRIFICE		GREAT SACRIFICE

With whom have you shared the gospel? On the same scale above, mark how great of a sacrifice it required by drawing a stick figure of yourself.

Now write the name of a person with whom you have felt prompted to share the gospel on the chart, indicating how great the sacrifice feels to you at the thought of it.

Now write Paul's name on the chart indicating how great of a sacrifice you believe he made in sharing the gospel.

Pause for a few moments and ponder how much the gospel has cost you in your lifetime. Record below anything the Holy Spirit reveals to you.

There is no doubt in my mind that Paul is encouraged to encounter these believers at Puteoli. I wonder what the Roman soldiers guarding Paul thought of all of this. One more question to save for heaven!

Paul becomes even more encouraged in the next few days.

What did the Roman believers do that greatly encouraged Paul?

Where did Paul live when they finally arrived within Rome?

Members of the Roman church traveled no less than forty-five miles to meet Paul. (Three Taverns was thirty-three miles south of Rome, and the Forum of Appius was ten miles south of that, so about forty-three miles from Rome.) No wonder he was encouraged—what affirmation! Upon his arrival, Paul got to work in his usual fashion—reaching out to his fellow Jews with the message of salvation.

How long did it take for Paul to summon his Jewish brethren?

What did Paul want to be sure his Jewish brothers understood in regard to his feelings about them?

For what reason did Paul insist he was on trial?

How did the Jewish people respond to Paul's report about himself and his trial?

How long did Paul spend expounding upon the Scriptures with the Jews in Rome?

How did some respond to Paul's message of salvation in Jesus? How did others respond?

According to Paul, for what reason had the message of salvation been sent to the Gentiles?

For how long did Paul remain in Rome? How did he make use of his time there?

Write out Acts 28:31 here:

Unlike many other towns in which Paul preached the gospel, it appears the Jews did not try to stop him in Rome. He was able to preach "without hindrance." This is one time his Jewish brothers did not try to stop his message. So while it may seem as though Luke ends rather abruptly from our point of view, from his standpoint of the spread of the gospel, this is a perfect ending.

Write out Acts 1:8:

At this time in history, Rome is pretty much considered the center of civilization or the "end of the earth." Paul had preached the gospel throughout the empire. It has spread as far south as Egypt, as far north as Bithynia and Macedonia and as far east as Syria. Opposition had come against the church of Jesus Christ from within its own walls and from without: Jews, Greeks, and the mighty Roman government. Yet in spite of it all, God protected His church and the gospel message continued to spread. Through ways and means Paul would never have believed if he had been told ahead of time, God orchestrated his movements and protected him, allowing the message to spread farther and farther.

You and I, however, know Rome is hardly the "end of the earth." There is a whole new yet-to-be-discovered world out there. This is what we'll discuss on our last day together.

A FINAL LEGACY

ACTS 29

You may have been confused by today's Scripture reading, wondering if there was something missing in your Bible. No, there is no Acts 29. Acts 28:31 is the end of Luke's story, but it's not the end of mine or yours.

Write out Acts 28:31 here:

Now write your name at the beginning of the sentence.

Your story is Acts 29. And mine. And every member of the unexplainable church who calls himself or herself by the name "Christian." And since this story has not yet been fully written, you and I get to decide how it ends.

When my daughter was little, she had a book titled *Milo and the Magical Stones* by Marcus Pfister. Milo was a mouse who lived on an island along with his other mice friends and a wise ruler named Balthazar. Life on their rocky island was good, except in the winter when the wind from the sea made their lives dark and cold. One day, however, Milo found a magical stone. It glowed with light and warmth, breaking through the hopelessly dark and dismal winter, bringing comfort and joy to all those who saw it. The other mice wanted a stone like Milo's and sought to find one for themselves. Balthazar warned that the stones did not belong to the mice, they belonged to the island, and if the mice took something that had been given as a gift, they needed to give a gift in return.

At this point in the story something unique happens. The author splits the pages in half and provides two different endings: one a happy ending and the other, a sad tale of woe. The two endings are stacked one on top of the other and the reader experiences both outcomes.

In the happy ending, Milo finds another stone and carves a beautiful sun on it and shares it with the island. The other mice also find their own magical stones and make beautiful carvings to share with the island in return. They live happily ever after in the warm glow of light provided by the magical stones and come together nightly for a beautiful parade in gratefulness for their new-found treasure.

In the sad ending, however, they greedily dig up the magical stones and provide no gifts in return. They begin to argue about whose stone is prettiest and best and they take more and more of them until the entire island is hollowed out from all of their digging. A giant wave washes over their island and the mice are carried away, with only Milo and Balthazar left.

My daughter, Eliana, never liked this book. Whenever we read it she would always look up at me with her big, brown eyes and say, "But which ending is real, Mama?" And I would reply, "Which one do you want to be real?" She would adamantly shake her head and say, "No, which one is ACTUALLY how it ended?" She did not like how the author had made her choose the ending. It felt to her that if the outcome were her personal decision, somehow that made it less real.

Maybe you can relate to that feeling. Maybe it feels like too much responsibility to write the end of your story. The end of the gospel story. The need to take up the message for this leg of the journey, the Acts 29 portion of the story. I understand that. The weight feels daunting at times, doesn't it? I begin to understand what Jesus meant when He said, "Deny yourself, take up your cross and follow me!" Crosses are heavy and sometimes exhausting to carry, especially when I don't know for how long and for what distance I'm being asked to carry it. The mystery of the divine invitation holds adventure, but also fear of the unknown.

But the truth is that we *have* been called to carry it. Paul passed the baton of the gospel to those coming after him and they picked it up and finished their race well. For countless generations. Until it reached you and me. And now we hold the baton—or shall we say—the divine invitation? So how does the story end from here? Do we carry it faithfully? Do we drop it? Do we greedily guard it, basking in the warmth and light it provides in our lives, thankful that we have it, yet unwilling to share it? Are we unwilling to return the gift we have graciously been given by sharing it with others?

I previously mentioned how my husband and I were in Turkey this past year with a group from our church. We toured the cities in which the seven churches of Revelation had stood. Six of these churches had been planted from the explosive growth of the Christian church in Ephesus under Paul's ministry. The area where all of those churches stand today is nearly 99 percent Muslim. Let that sink in for a moment. Remnants of the gospel in Turkey remain carved in stones lying in ruins. Most passerby tourists may not even notice the Christian symbols as they walk by them. Somehow, at some point, somebody dropped the baton. Or guarded it greedily. And the gospel in Turkey has been largely swept away in the sands of time. Tucked within their beautiful countryside a few followers of Jesus continue to press on fighting the good fight of faith under a government growing increasingly Muslim in social practice. Oh, I'm sure there is a Milo and a Balthazar somewhere, shaking their head in disbelief at what has become of their beautiful homeland. But the rest of the mice are gone. The unexplainable church lives on, but not with the same vibrancy as in days gone by.

So what about us? In our time? We hold the light of truth. We can hide ourselves in our homes and church buildings, basking in the beauty and warmth of our redemption, or we can share the gift in return. We can ensure that the unexplainable church stands tall and shines brightly in our corner of the world, in our generation, or we can rely on somebody else and worry about it later. We decide the end of the story.

Too much responsibility, you say? Too daunting? Beyond our ability? Ah yes, to all three. But to the Holy Spirit who lives inside of us? This is what He lives for! This is why He was given to us. To carry forth the gospel in and through the unexplainable church. So what is the ACTUAL ending?

The divine invitation begins at the moment of surrender—when you and I resolve to follow Jesus wherever He may lead. When the realization occurs that the unexplainable church needs you to carry on and you need the church for your divine invitation to be carried out—this is when your invitation has been opened and you have officially RSVP'd to the grandest adventure of your life. You and I are members of a kingdom——the unexplainable church—that is so much bigger than ourselves, and it exists for the glory of our King.

Before you close your book for one last time today, sit prayerfully at the feet of our King and write out your own Acts 29 ending below:

Paul writes in 1 Corinthians 9:24, "Do you not know that in a race all the runners run, but only one receives the prize? So run that you may obtain it." It's time to lace up those shoes, my friend. There's a great, big, yet-to-be-discovered world out there. Finish well. Your crown is waiting.

PAUL'S ACTS 29 STORY

I would imagine you might be wondering, "Whatever happened to Paul after his two-year imprisonment in Rome?" Truthfully, much of what happened after that time is widely debated. We mentioned that prisoners under Roman law were typically held for a period of two years. If their accusers did not bring them to trial within that time period, the case generally was dropped and they were released. A Roman citizen could not be convicted until they had the opportunity to face their accusers. The text intimates that at the end of two years, something changed in Paul's situation.

During his two-year imprisonment, Paul wrote his letters to Ephesus, Philippi, Colossae, and Philemon. In these letters he presents confidence that he will be acquitted or released by emperor Nero. In Philippians 1 he claims that he is confident he will remain for the continued strengthening of the churches, and in Philippians 2 he says he is confident that he will be able to personally visit them soon. Six or seven years later, he appears to directly reference his trial before Nero stating, "At my first defense no one came to stand by me, but all deserted me. May it not be charged against them! But the Lord stood by me and strengthened me, so that through me the message might be fully proclaimed and all the Gentiles might hear it" (2 Timothy 4:16–17).

So what happened during the six-year period after his release and a subsequent arrest, trial, and death under the same emperor? Well, Paul's statement above gives us an inkling of an idea. During his two-year imprisonment, he didn't feel that the message had yet been fully proclaimed and that "all the Gentiles" had heard it. So presumably, after Paul's release, he set about preaching again. But where did he go exactly?

Some people believe he went to Spain, citing Romans 15:24 in which he wrote about his desire to go there. The historian Eusebius supports Paul's travels to Spain, as do early church fathers Jerome and Chrysostom. Others, however, disagree and piece together personal remarks from his epistles to construct an alternative route, revisiting his previously established churches, including Crete (Titus 1:5), Miletus and Corinth (2 Timothy 4:20), Troas (2 Timothy 4:13), Nicopolis (Titus 3:12), along with Philippi and Colossae (1 Timothy 1:3), concluding there was not enough time for him to travel to Spain before his final imprisonment and execution in Rome. If, after reading the last sentence, you get the feeling that it's a bit of an inconclusive timeline, we're on the same page.

I often feel that what God doesn't explicitly tell us is just as important as what He does. Where Paul went after Acts 28 may pique our curiosity, but it's not integral to our carrying forth the unexplainable church. Once Paul reached Rome and became imprisoned there, he was able to mentor future church leaders, write four New Testament epistles, and prepare the churches for the next wave of church history. He had fought the good fight and finished his race. It was now time for others like Timothy, John Mark, John, Luke, Aristarchus, Trophimus, and countless others to run with it. In these final epistles, Paul charges them to preach the word, teach sound doctrine, continue worshiping in community, establish strong leaders, pray for all people, and keep the faith. Paul says of himself, "Henceforth there is laid up for me the crown of righteousness, which the Lord, the righteous judge, will award to me on that day, and not only to me but also to all who have loved his appearing" (2 Timothy 4:8).

Paul approached death with confidence that he had finished well. While tradition tells us Paul was beheaded on the Ostian Road outside of Rome, his Acts 29 was a happy ending. He ran the race that had been marked out for him. His race. And his prayer for every believer behind him was to finish their own. Within our soul we carry the unexplainable church—the message of Jesus Christ, who came to save sinners, redeem the world, and bring us all to glory. Now it's our race. Are you ready? Within your heart and hands you hold a divine invitation, my friend. One written for you before time began, etched into eternity and sealed with the shed blood of your Savior. The Spirit is beckoning you to the starting block. This is your time. This is your race. On your mark, get set, GO!

NOTES

1. The law given to Moses had so many regulations that it was virtually impossible to not break any. Sins committed without a person realizing it were unintentional sins. Because of God's perfect holiness, even these sins needed to be atoned for, and in His graciousness, He prescribed a way: the animal sacrifices under the law provided the offering to cleanse the sinner. But under Levitical Law, there was no sacrifice for sins that were committed deliberately, willfully, rebelliously. Various penalties, rather than animal sacrifices, were exacted for intentional sin.

   The Old Testament system of offering for sin foreshadowed the sacrifice of Jesus, whose shed blood on the cross covers all sins—past, present, future, willful, unintended—of those who accept His sacrifice on their behalf.

   Does this mean we should take sin lightly, or willfully sin because "I'll be forgiven anyway"? Of course not, as Romans 6:1 states. Sin must be taken very seriously. Will we struggle with our bent toward sin? Certainly! Even Paul admitted his frustration with his sin nature; see Romans 7:15. But we accept with gratitude Christ's atonement for all our sins, and we cooperate with the Holy Spirit as we continue to grow to be more like Him (John 15:4–5; Rom. 12:1–2; 2 Cor. 3:18).

2. Spiros Zodhiates, trans. *The Hebrew-Greek Key Study Bible* (Grand Rapids: Baker Book House, 1984), 1683.

3. Ibid., 1684.

4. H.A. Ironside, *Acts* (Grand Rapids: Kregel, 2007), 208.

5. John R.W. Stott, *The Message of Acts* (Downers Grove, IL: IVP Academic, 1990), 265.

6. Ironside, *Acts*, 211.

7. Stott, *The Message of Acts*, 266.

8. Chuck Smith, *The Book of Acts* (Costa Mesa, CA: The Word for Today, 2013), 272.

9. N.T. Wright, *Acts for Everyone Part 2* (Louisville: Westminster John Knox Press, 2008), 84.

10. Stott, *The Message of Acts*, 280–81.

11. N.T. Wright, *Acts for Everyone Part 2*, 91.

12. John F. Walvoord and Roy B. Zuck, *The Bible Knowledge Commentary New Testament* (Colorado Springs: David C. Cook, 1983), 413.

13. William H. Marty, "Acts" in *The Moody Bible Commentary*, Michael Rydelnik and Michael Vanlaningham, gen. eds. (Chicago: Moody, 2014), 1724.

14. Craig S. Keener, *The IVP Bible Background Commentary New Testament* (Downer's Grove, IL: Intervarsity Press, 2014), 397.

15. Ibid, 780.

16. Stott, *The Message of Acts*, 364.

17. Keener, *The IVP Bible Background Commentary New Testament*, 408.

18. Ibid., 414.

ACKNOWLEDGMENTS

I always hesitate with this section, because truthfully there is not a person I know who has not contributed to this story in some way, either as a follower of Jesus or not. There are, however, certain individuals who must be mentioned by name.

The Author and Perfecter of the Unexplainable Church: Jesus Christ, Almighty God Incarnate, at whose feet I cast this work in awe that You would allow me to write it.

My family: Jonathan, Eliana, and Nathan, whom I love more than life itself. You have sacrificed much to allow these pages to be written. Thank you for believing in this call to complete this work.

My pastor, Steve Engram, who shepherds his flock with a beautiful balance of truth and grace. I am forever grateful that God brought our family under your leadership and spiritual authority.

My prayer warriors who were always just a text or a post away and kept me going when this runner grew weary.

Judy Dunagan, whose heart beats for the unexplainable church with the rhythm of her Savior. Thank you for allowing me to run all the way to Acts 29 and being a faithful guide and pacesetter.

To Pam Pugh, whose editing and careful attention to detail carried this work across the finish line with beauty and grace. Your way with words communicates the heart of Christ and I am humbled and grateful for your willingness to mold and shape this work to make it more reflective of Him.

To every runner out there who has joined this team called the Unexplainable Church, let us throw off everything that hinders and the sin that so easily entangles and run the race marked out for us. Thank you for allowing me to be a part of this leg of your journey. I'm humbled and honored to run alongside you. See you at the finish line, friend!

A D R I A T I C S E A

BULGARIA

MACEDONIA

MACEDONIA

ALBANIA

Thessalonica
Berea
Amphipolis
Apollonia
Philippi
Neapolis
THASOS
SAMOTHR

GREECE

AEGEAN SEA

LEMNOS

SKIROS

EVVOIA

Rome
Three Taverns
Forum of Appius
Puteoli

ITALY

Delphi
A C H A I A
Corinth
Cenchreae
Athens

Sparta

Rhegium

SICILY

I O N I A N S E A

Syracuse

SANTOR

MALTA

CRETE
Phoenix
Las
CAUDA
Fair
Havens

M   E   D   I   T   E   R   R   A   N   E

Cyrene

CYRENAICA

●	City
⊙	Addressee of Pauline Epistle
▲	Mountain peak
≍	Mountain pass
LYCIA	Roman provincial or regional name

AFRICA

0   50   100   150 Miles

0   50   100   150   200 Kilometers